SOCIAL PRINCIPLES

of

The United Methodist Church 2017-2020

With official text and teaching exercises,
plus Our Social Creed

This book is produced for
The United Methodist Church
by The United Methodist Publishing House
in cooperation with the General Board of Church & Society
100 Maryland Avenue NE, Washington DC 20002
202-488-5600
www.umcjustice.org
gbcs@gbcs.org

Contents

INTRODUCTION
TO THE SOCIAL PRINCIPLES

The Social Principles are a good faith response to what we believe God is already doing in our lives and in the public square. They are an expression of the common ground we share, reflecting our priorities and helping us learn about and advocate for vulnerable peoples and a vulnerable planet. The Social Principles express The United Methodist Church's official positions on societal issues, casting a vision for a just and equitable world.

Even though the Social Principles are "church words," their language may not be familiar to every member of The United Methodist Church. Part of our responsibility as members of the church is to unpack the Social Principles and to amplify what they actually mean in our own context and in the diverse contexts across the world.

The preface to the Social Principles emphasizes that they are "instructive and persuasive in the best of the prophetic spirit." The Social Principles can be clearly marked signposts on our journey toward living fully into God's gracious love for the world; they give us clear direction. Sometimes, though, we may experience the Social Principles as a kind of road map on which the terrain is familiar but some twists and turns are strange to us. Once we orient ourselves to this new geography, we are able to explore the course we are to take. The Social Principles may also show us how far we have come as a church as we look back at the ground we've covered. As United Methodists, we covenant to be a connectional church, to travel together even in the midst of our diversity, periodically adjusting our road map and, hopefully, moving closer toward God's vision for our world.

John Wesley invested in relationships with people most affected by societal inequities, making ministry to the poor or otherwise vulnerable a priority in the Methodist movement. Wesley pointed to the oppressive causes and effects of systemic poverty and forged personal friendships with impoverished and neglected people. He promoted equity in health care, sustainable economic development, sustainable food production and distribution, access to a clean environment, and equitable access to education. He spoke out against abuses such as expanding imperialism and colonialism, mass incarceration, and human trafficking; he promoted religious tolerance and the dignity and sacred worth of indigenous peoples. These emphases illustrate the prophetic ministry of the early Methodist movement, responding to God's grace working in and on behalf of a wounded world. The Social Principles are a faithful and fresh expression of our Wesleyan missional mandate "to make disciples of Jesus Christ for the transformation of the world," or, as Wesley articulates, our call "to reform the nation, particularly the church, and to spread scriptural holiness over the land" (¶ 120; "Minutes of Several Conversations" Q.3, in *The Works of John Wesley* [vol. 8; ed. T. Jackson; Baker, 1978], 299).

The placement of the Social Principles between "The Ministry of All Christians" and "Organization and Administration" in the 2016 *Discipline* reminds us that we cannot engage in ministry and mission without also engaging society and its ills collectively. While personal choices, habits, and commitments do change the world, organizations and structures provide us with a concrete means by which we live out our faith, seek justice, and pursue peace in ways that we cannot accomplish on our own. The Social Principles urge us not only to make a difference in the world but also (and as urgently) to build a different kind of world than the one in which we live.

As you read through the Social Principles, you may find yourself enthusiastically nodding in agreement, or you may vehemently disagree. Many people may feel overjoyed when they discover that what their conscience and their lived experience has taught them is actually in accord with the Social Principles, and others, even lifelong United Methodists, may genuinely feel defensive when a portion of the Social Principles sounds as if it is in conflict with their core convictions. You might even find yourself surprised to discover a topic you had not thought about very much. Perhaps your curiosity will lead you to explore such an issue in greater depth.

WHERE DO I START?

The 2016 *Discipline* describes the Social Principles as "a prayerful and thoughtful effort on the part of the General Conference to speak to the human issues in the contemporary world from a sound biblical and theological foundation" (see preface to the Social Principles). The Social Principles are a catalyst for and a product of prayer. The Social Principles begin with holy conferencing by people of faith at General Conference, but they must be lived throughout the connection to have lasting value.

Read through the Social Principles and take a moment to consider from whom you first learned the principles that would guide your life. Was this a parent, grandparent, teacher, pastor, or neighbor? How have these ideals shaped your life? Ask yourself prayerfully, "Have there been instances where I was persuaded by someone's story, a new experience in my life, or by information I had not yet been exposed to that caused me to modify my perspective, to cultivate a different perspective, or to reevaluate a once firmly held conviction?"

As you pray, study, discuss, and put into practice the Social Principles, allow them to ease you into a "prayerful, studied dialogue" with yourself, your communities, your church, and God (see preface). You may find yourself beginning to critically and constructively question some principles that at one time seemed unquestionably clear to you and to appreciate new principles that at one time seemed unrelated to you.

WHERE DO THE SOCIAL PRINCIPLES COME FROM?

The Social Principles, spanning ¶¶ 160-166 in the *Book of Discipline*, connect The United Methodist Church as we express our faith in collaborative practice. As more than 43,000 local churches and 12.8 million United Methodists in the United States, Africa, Central and Southeast Asia, and Europe, we hold the Social Principles in common across our many diverse cultures, ethnicities, and national identities. At their best, the Social Principles articulate our ethical aspirations for the common good in our public policies and personal commitments. Through them, we seek to love God with our whole heart, mind, soul, and strength and to desire for our neighbors what we desire for ourselves.

The United Methodist Church publicly and officially speaks about social issues through the Social Principles as adopted by the General Conference. Additional legislated statements approved by the General Conference, included in *The Book of Discipline of The United Methodist Church* and *The Book of Resolutions of The United Methodist Church* are anchored in our Social Principles. Only the

General Conference, the church's highest policy-making body, has the authority to change the language in the Social Principles.

From the beginning, The United Methodist Church affirmed the gospel of Jesus Christ to be both social and personal. The predecessor to the Social Principles was written in 1908 and took the form of a Social Creed. The Social Creed was the first document of its kind written by a church. It was drafted during a historic period of rapid rural displacement and relocation, mass national migration, and unchecked corporate greed and industrial urbanization. Refusing to ignore that society was in the midst of social change, The Methodist Episcopal Church took the opportunity to act, illustrating these changing realities and seeking to respond in faith:

> A young Irish girl named Maureen began work at the age of 14 in a woolen mill in Lawrence, MA. Beginning at six o'clock every morning she swept and cleaned the mill floor. For this task Maureen was paid $3.50 for a 56-hour week, ten cents of which went for drinking water from a polluted canal. While working, she saw many older workers seriously injured by the dangerous mill machinery because of being forced to work so fast. Maureen and her family who had left Ireland to escape famine all lived in one room in a boarding house. Lunch and supper everyday consisted of black bread, molasses, and beans. On Sunday hopefully there was a piece of meat.

The Social Gospel movement, evangelical at its heart and inspired by Jesus' preaching of "the kingdom of God," was acutely aware of the brutality of deplorable working conditions, the social tensions arising from assimilating millions of European migrants, shifting cultural values, increases in addiction, inequitable economic practices in rapidly growing urban centers, and neglected rural regions in the United States. This movement advocated for a day of Sabbath rest, a living wage for workers, an end to sweatshop child labor, and recognition of human dignity and rights for persons marginalized by oppressive class divisions.

Inspired by the Wesleyan Methodist Union, recently organized in England, and the community organizing efforts of Methodist suffragettes Jane Addams and Mary McDowell, five Methodist Episcopal clergy established the Methodist Federation for Social Service. They included evangelist Frank Mason North from the New York Conference, author of the seminal Methodist hymn "Where Cross the Crowded Ways of Life"; Ohio Wesleyan University president, Herbert Welch; publishing house editor Elbert Robb Zaring; and

Cleveland pastor Worth Tippy and Chicago pastor Harry F. Ward, both of whom had officiated at far too many untimely funerals for meat packinghouse workers killed because of unsafe and inhumane factory working conditions.

Workers lacked advocates and a just means to organize and were ground down by fourteen-hour shifts and seven-day work-weeks. Families were broken apart by absent or exhausted parents. Disabled workers were summarily dismissed; those who retired were left without a pension or health care; and children worked when they should have been at school or at play. At the same time, enormous wealth was generated and distributed primarily to factory owners, not the workers who made such production possible.

The new Social Creed was an eleven-point call to action presented as a platform at the General Conference. It became a public rallying cry for the church to live up to the demands of the gospel and to advocate for justice in the public square; it called for society to reform itself in light of the example of Christ.

The Methodist Episcopal Church stands:

- For equal rights and complete justice for all men in all stations of life.
- For the principles of conciliation and arbitration in industrial dissensions.
- For the protection of the worker from dangerous machinery, occupational diseases, injuries and mortality.
- For the abolition of child labor.
- For such regulation of the conditions of labor for women as shall safeguard the physical and moral health of the community.
- For the suppression of the "sweating system."
- For the gradual and reasonable reduction of the hours of labor to the lowest practical point, with work for all; and for that degree of leisure for all which is the condition of the highest human life.
- For a release for [from] employment one day in seven.
- For a living wage in every industry.
- For the highest wage that each industry can afford, and for the most equitable division of the products of industry that can ultimately be devised.

- For the recognition of the Golden Rule and the mind of Christ as the supreme law of society and the sure remedy for all social ills.

The Social Creed, which was first drafted on a Western Union notepad, was adopted without dissent on May 30, 1908, by the General Conference meeting in Baltimore, Maryland.

One-fourth of that General Conference's Episcopal Address was devoted to social justice (particularly to issues of child labor and the union movement) and the means by which the church ought to alleviate systemic poverty. Subsequently, the 1908 Social Creed was presented at the White House to President Theodore Roosevelt. Genuinely Wesleyan and thoroughly ecumenical, the Social Creed was adopted by the Federal Council of Churches (now the National Council of Churches of Christ in the USA) within two years of its initial publication.

HOW ABOUT THE 1972 SOCIAL CREED?

The two predecessor denominations to The United Methodist Church, The Evangelical United Brethren and The Methodist Church, brought to their union two distinct statements on social issues, "The Methodist Social Creed" of The Methodist Church and "Basic Beliefs Regarding Social Issues and Moral Standards" of The Evangelical United Brethren Church. Both creeds trace their origin to the first 1908 Social Creed, and although each was written with a particular audience in mind, together they presented the new church with a substantial mandate.

In 1968, these two statements were printed sequentially in the first United Methodist *Discipline* under the new heading "Social Principles" with a preface explaining their common history and basic agreement. Bishop James S. Thomas, who chaired the Commission on Social Principles to rewrite the Social Creed, expressed the prevalent ethos and opportunity of that time: "The world is literally hanging under the threat of extinction. Indeed, a sense of impending doom seems almost prerequisite to an ecclesial statement of social witness, many of which are born of a sense of crisis."

The 1972 General Conference shared Bishop Thomas' resolve by declaring in its first edition of new Social Creed and Social Principles that:

The [global] unity now being thrust upon us by technological revolution has far outrun our moral and spiritual capacity to achieve a stable world. . . . [presenting] the church as well as all people with problems that will not wait for answers. . . . This generation must find viable answers to these and related questions if humanity is to continue on this earth.

The title "Social Principles" was used for the first time in 1972. It included the six major sections we have today and concluded with the new Social Creed. The General Conference asked that "Our Social Creed" be read regularly in every congregation and used frequently in Sunday worship services. In 2008, the General Conference approved "A Companion Litany to Our Social Creed" (found in ¶ 166) to be used especially in services of worship. The new litany was the result of several consultations on four continents, hosted by United Methodists in the Philippines, Norway, the United States, and the Democratic Republic of the Congo, with input from across the worldwide church.

The Social Principles have evolved over time. The 2016 Social Principles, like the 1972 Social Principles, still reflect our common theological task to be at once critical and constructive, individual and communal, contextual and practical (¶ 105). They demonstrate, in carefully articulated words, our commitments to and our relationships with the people who are most directly impacted by urgent social issues. The Social Principles reflect forthright opposition to specific choices and public policies, mediated agreements on a variety of positions, and clear affirmation of practices that favor justice, reconciliation, and peace.

When we are in meaningful, mutual relationships with others, the Social Principles and the Social Creed become far more than any one position we may take as a church—they become crucial illustrations of how we incarnate and embody the gospel in an ever more globalized, pluralistic church and society today.

THE SOCIAL PRINCIPLES AS AN
INTEGRATED DOCUMENT

The Social Principles are placed into seven paragraphs or sections, spanning ¶¶ 160-166: The Natural World, The Nurturing Community, The Social Community, The Economic Community, The Political Community, The World Community, and Our Social Creed. The Social Principles elaborate on specific timely issues, and they are intrinsically connected. Reading only one social principle without reading the others can limit their collective importance.

The Social Principles are intersectional. For example, The Natural World does not exist independent of the issues addressed in The Economic Community; concerns lifted up in The Social Community are also embedded in our discussion of The World Community; the section on The Political Community reflects the yearnings we describe in The Nurturing Community; and the rights, privileges and responsibilities discussed in The Social Community have implications for how we understand ourselves as part of The Natural World.

We live in multiple communities at once and are continually shaped by all of the Social Principles. Just as our faith cannot be separated from our day-to-day life choices, it is difficult to look at only one social issue without considering its impact on other social issues. It is preferable to take time to cross-reference each section as you study the Social Principles and become familiar with them all.

Remember that the Social Principles are not only the product of the General Conference, the highest legislative body of The United Methodist Church. They are also an invitation for all members of the church and society to be formed anew by making consistent and deliberate decisions that will align their attitudes, habits, choices, and social structures with the mind of Christ and the will of God for the common good.

Only the General Conference can officially speak for The United Methodist Church. Individuals, local churches, conferences, general agencies, and caucuses may make policy statements or offer their assessment of an urgent issue that has not been addressed by the General Conference, but these bodies cannot offer any official position in the name of The United Methodist Church beyond those stated in the *Book of Discipline* and the *Book of Resolutions*. In this sense, the Social Principles do not reflect the will of one part of the church; they are an expression of the entire church body.

THE SOCIAL PRINCIPLES – POSITIONS, INTERESTS, VALUES, NEEDS

It may be helpful to look at each social principle as an expression of a public position that reflects a set of personal convictions. While you may not agree with each of the Social Principles, they are a solid starting point for further dialogue.

Positions determined by fair, transparent, and representative legislative processes tell us where the church finds itself today: what it stands for and what it opposes. Our positions determine what we will see. With whom we will stand influences the kind of transformative education, advocacy, and organizing with which we will respond. It may be helpful to think of the Social Principles as positional norms or standards by which we measure how closely we live up to the church's vision for a just society, a society based on right relationships with one another and our neighbors. Ask yourself, "Are my personal positions informed and shaped by the Social Principles? How or how not?"

The Social Principles reflect the sincere interests of particular groups in the church and in society. Our interests are shaped by our life experience, the company we keep, the work we do, the people with whom we live and worship, those with whom we stand in solidarity, and those who we call our friends. It is important to know that in several places the Social Principles reflect both the particular interests of marginalized, vulnerable, and neglected peoples and places and the church's desire to realign society's interests in ways that will increase these populations' capacity to flourish. Consider how the interests you represent actually align with the interests articulated in the Social Principles.

The Social Principles make reference to many values we cherish and promote as a church. These beliefs define us as United Methodists and as Christians. They include values such as justice, mutuality, respect, security, freedom, responsibility, and the sacred worth and dignity of all people. As you read the Social Principles, consider these prominent values and the way they inform our growth in personal and social holiness as Christians and as a church.

The Social Principles are a response to the pressing needs we see among people and for the planet today. We practice a living faith that is both personal and public, one we express in acts of mercy and justice that seek to meet the needs of people and the planet. These needs may be as basic as food, shelter, air, security, and care. Regardless of the groups with which we identify, the values to which we aspire, or the positions we publicly represent, we have basic needs. Consider the consequences to our church, society, and planet when these needs are left unaddressed or unmet.

Each local church is unique, yet it is a part of a connection, a living organism we describe as the body of Christ. Living as a connectional church means that every local United Methodist church is interrelated through the structure and organization of districts, conferences, and jurisdictions in the larger "family" of the denomination. Our church extends far beyond your doorstep, with both a local and an international presence; we are truly a worldwide church with a prophetic set of positions, interests, values, and needs.

HOW DOES THE CHURCH SPEAK THROUGH THE SOCIAL PRINCIPLES?

By adopting the Social Principles, the General Conference has officially spoken on a wide range of social issues for and to The United Methodist Church. As our church's "Doctrinal Standards and Our Theological Task" explain, "The Social Principles (¶¶ 160-166) provide our most recent official summary of stated convictions that seek to apply the Christian vision of righteousness to social, economic, and political issues" (¶ 102).

You might find it helpful to think of the Social Principles as a document developed by a large committee. The highest legislative body in The United Methodist Church is the General Conference. The voting membership consists of an equal number of clergy delegates and lay delegates. Both clergy and laity have one vote. Bishops in The United Methodist Church preside over legislative committees but cannot vote at General Conference.

The General Conference convenes every four years. (This four-year period is known as a quadrennium.) It is the only body that can speak officially for the church. The General Conference is composed of no more than one thousand delegates elected by various conferences in The United Methodist Church. The 2016 General Conference represented the 12.8 million-member United Methodist Church with 58% of delegates from the U.S., 30% from Africa, 4.6% from Europe, and 5.5% from the Philippines.

Every four years, any member, local church, conference, caucus, or general agency within The United Methodist Church may petition the General Conference to change any part of *The Book of Discipline of The United Methodist Church,* including the Social Principles. Prior to each General Conference, thousands of petitions are sent to the Secretary of the General Conference. Many of these petitions deal with some portion of the Social Principles.

At the beginning of the General Conference's session, most petitions relating to the Social Principles are given to the General Conference's Standing Legislative Committees on Church and Society. Delegates in these two legislative committees divide further into smaller groups (subcommittees) to consider and make recommendations on each petition. The Standing Legislative Committees, acting on the recommendations of their subcommittees, deliberate and vote on these petitions, presenting their recommendations to the entire General Conference. The General Conference then accepts, amends, refers, or defeats these petitions. Once adopted by the General Conference, a petition becomes the official statement of The United Methodist Church.

Only in recent years has the General Conference formally addressed such issues as the privatization of water resources, global climate change, sexual harassment and sexual assault, media violence, and corruption. These join our church's long-standing historic positions in favor of a living wage for all, radical hospitality toward immigrants and migrants, health care as a basic human right, abundant health through abstinence from tobacco and alcohol, and our opposition to capital punishment and mass incarceration.

Delegates to the 2016 General Conference held in Portland, Oregon, made significant changes to most paragraphs of the Social Principles. These were substantial additions, deletions, or amendments reflecting new or revised positions in the church. Consider these new social principles, the timely interests they promote, the values they reflect, and the unmet needs they seek to meet. New content was added to three paragraphs.

In accordance with growing societal awareness of bullying, a new section has been added that "encourages churches to adopt a policy of zero tolerance for bullying, including cyberbullying," and affirms "the right of all people regardless of gender, socioeconomic status, race, religion, disability, age, physical appearance, sexual orientation and gender identity to be free of unwanted aggressive behavior and harmful control tactics." This new social principle stands alongside several other social principles addressing the sacred worth of all persons and our church's opposition to violence (¶ 161R).

Focusing our attention on recovery and healing of all persons, the "Family Violence and Abuse" section now includes a call for the church and society "to work with the abuser to understand the root causes and forms of abuse and to overcome such behaviors," as "regardless of the cause or the abuse, both the victim and the abuser need the love of the Church. While we deplore the actions of the abuser, we affirm that person to be in need of God's redeeming love" (¶ 161H).

For the first time, the Social Principles include a statement on pornography: "We oppose all forms of pornography and consider its use a form of sexual misconduct. Pornography is sexually explicit material that portrays violence, abuse, coercion, domination, humiliation, or degradation for the purpose of sexual arousal" (¶ 161Q).

Also new to the Social Principles is a section on "Culture and Identity" which states: "We affirm that no identity or culture has more legitimacy than any other. We call the Church to challenge any hierarchy of cultures or identities. Through relationships within and among cultures we are called to and have the responsibility for learning from each other, showing mutual respect for our differences and similarities as we experience the diversity of perspectives and viewpoints" (¶ 161A). With its focus on the integrity of distinct cultures in a pluralistic society, this principle complements our current positions on race and ethnicity.

Additionally, five principles were amended at the 2016 General Conference.

The amended section on "Rights of Racial and Ethnic Persons" makes explicit the church's awareness of and response to white privilege: "In many cultures white persons are granted unearned privileges and benefits that are denied to persons of color. We oppose the creation of a racial hierarchy in any culture. Racism breeds racial discrimination." Further, "we commit as the Church to move beyond symbolic expressions and representative models that do not challenge unjust systems of power and access" (¶ 162A). This social principle clearly names how privilege undermines the intentions of the Gospel.

"Rights of Immigrants" was amended to read, "We oppose immigration policies that separate family members from each other or that include detention of families with children, and we call on local churches to be in ministry with immigrant families" (¶ 162H). This principle recommits the church to advocate for the integrity of families and our role as Christians to provide welcome and outreach to all persons.

"Basic Freedoms and Human Rights" now additionally affirms that "blockades and embargoes that seek to impede the flow or free commerce of food and medicines are practices that cause pain and suffering, malnutrition, or starvation with all its detrimental consequences to innocent and noncombatant civilian populations, especially children. We reject these as instruments of domestic and foreign policy regardless of political or ideological views"

(¶ 164*A*). In this statement, we prioritize our commitment to meeting human needs, especially in settings of escalating conflict between nations.

Reflecting the increasing complexity of broken relationships, the section on "Divorce" was amended to read, "The church must be on the forefront of premarital, marital, and postmarital counseling in order to create and preserve healthy relationships" (¶ 161*D*).

Lastly, "Ministry with Those Who Have Experienced Abortion" was amended to add, "We commit our Church to continue to provide nurturing ministries to those who terminate a pregnancy, to those in the midst of a crisis pregnancy, and to those who give birth" (¶ 161*K*). This change elaborates on our commitment as the Church to be in ministry with all persons.

Consider these new 2016 social principles alongside the former ones. If you discover a new principle that you, your youth group, Sunday school class, administrative council, caucus, or another group within The United Methodist Church believes should be included in the Social Principles, you may send a petition to be acted upon at the 2020 General Conference. If you would like to learn more about submitting a petition to the General Conference, your pastor or district superintendent will be able to offer you further guidance.

At the 2020 General Conference, the Social Principles will likely see significant revision. As requested by the 2012 General Conference, the General Board of Church and Society has engaged in a years-long process to revise the Social Principles to make them even more globally relevant, theologically founded, and succinct. Seven worldwide consultations have been held in Africa, Europe, the Philippines, and the United States. The 2016 General Conference affirmed this preparatory work, and the General Board of Church and Society will now undertake a revision process with the intention of proposing a modified set of Social Principles to the 2020 General Conference.

WHAT DIFFERENCE DO THE SOCIAL PRINCIPLES MAKE FOR ME?

You may find that someone you are close to, someone you care about, or even a new partner in ministry is directly impacted by one or more of the Social Principles. This could lead you to appreciate their life circumstances or their lived experiences in a new way. You may feel an urge to discover how a social principle affects them.

It could also be that you find some social principles at odds with your own lived experience and deeply held convictions. You may honestly hold beliefs that cannot easily be reconciled with one or more of the Social Principles. It would be natural to ask, "Do I need to accept all of the Social Principles in order to be a faithful member of The United Methodist Church?"

The practical answer is no. No one will come around with a copy of the 2017-2020 Social Principles and demand that you sign your name to the document to prove your loyalty to The United Methodist Church. The Church believes the Social Principles are "a call to faithfulness and are intended to be instructive and persuasive in the best of the prophetic spirit," and "a call to all members of The United Methodist Church to a prayerful, studied dialogue of faith and practice" (see preface).

We are to be in dialogue with and practice the Social Principles and to allow them to be instructional for us. At the same time, we are to exercise our conscience and take seriously the implications of our faith as Christians through the eyes of our prophetic tradition. In that same prophetic sense, the Social Principles can, should, and do challenge us to consider our attitudes and actions faithfully and critically.

The 2016 *Discipline* states, "The standards of attitude and conduct set forth in the Social Principles . . . shall be considered as an essential resource for guiding each member of the Church in being a servant of Christ on mission" (¶ 220). However, some provisions within the 2016 *Discipline* require particular persons and agencies of The United Methodist Church to conform their actions to the Social Principles in certain ways:

- *Lay leadership:* "Members of the church council or alternative structure shall be persons of genuine Christian character who love the church, are morally disciplined, are committed to the mandate of inclusiveness in the life of the church, are loyal to the ethical standards of The United Methodist Church set forth in the Social Principles, and are competent to administer its affairs"(¶ 244.3).
- *Outside organizations:* "When a pastor and/or a board of trustees are asked to grant permission to an outside organization to use church facilities, permission can be granted only when such use is consistent with the Social Principles (¶¶ 160-166) and ecumenical objectives" (¶ 2533.3).

- *Clergy and candidates:* Ordained ministers as well as candidates for ordination are expected to "assume a lifestyle consistent with Christian teaching as set forth in the Social Principles" (¶ 337.2).
- *Investments:* Boards of Trustees at every level of the church, from the local church through the general agencies, are encouraged to invest funds under their control in enterprises that "make a positive contribution toward the realization of the goals outlined in the Social Principles of The United Methodist Church" (¶ 1310). Investments, while maximizing funds for mission in a manner consistent with the preservation of capital, are to follow the Policies Relative to Socially Responsible Investments and the Social Principles of the Church (¶¶ 613.5, 717).
- *The General Board of Church and Society (GBCS):* GBCS, as well as related bodies in conferences and local churches that are tasked with ministries of church and society, seek to interpret and implement the Social Principles in good faith (¶ 1004).

Besides these provisions of law as found in the 2016 *Discipline,* the real question is, "What difference will I permit the Social Principles to make in my life, in the life of my congregation, and in the communities to which I relate?" The Social Principles are far more than a set of guidelines by which we agree to abide in accordance with the position we hold. The Social Principles reflect that which is important in our individual life stories and our collective story. In a very real sense, people's stories, passions, concerns, and priorities are mirrored in the Social Principles. Genuine reflection means we will make every effort to learn and appreciate the positions, interests, values, and needs that are found in our Church's collective story, locally and globally.

Part V
SOCIAL PRINCIPLES

PREFACE

The United Methodist Church has a long history of concern for social justice. Its members have often taken forthright positions on controversial issues involving Christian principles. Early Methodists expressed their opposition to the slave trade, to smuggling, and to the cruel treatment of prisoners.

A social creed was adopted by The Methodist Episcopal Church (North) in 1908. Within the next decade similar statements were adopted by The Methodist Episcopal Church, South, and by The Methodist Protestant Church. The Evangelical United Brethren Church adopted a statement of social principles in 1946 at the time of the uniting of the United Brethren and The Evangelical Church. In 1972, four years after the uniting in 1968 of The Methodist Church and The Evangelical United Brethren Church, the General Conference of The United Methodist Church adopted a new statement of Social Principles, which was revised in 1976 (and by each successive General Conference).

The Social Principles, while not to be considered church law,[1] are a prayerful and thoughtful effort on the part of the General Conference to speak to the human issues in the contemporary world from a sound biblical and theological foundation as historically demonstrated in United Methodist traditions. They are a call to faithfulness and are intended to be instructive and persuasive in the best of the prophetic spirit. The Social Principles are a call to all members of The United Methodist Church to a prayerful, studied dialogue of faith and practice. (See ¶ 509.)

---

1. See Judicial Council Decisions 833, 1254.

PREAMBLE

We, the people called United Methodists, affirm our faith in God our Creator and Father, in Jesus Christ our Savior, and in the Holy Spirit, our Guide and Guard.

We acknowledge our complete dependence upon God in birth, in life, in death, and in life eternal. Secure in God's love, we affirm the goodness of life and confess our many sins against God's will for us as we find it in Jesus Christ. We have not always been faithful stewards of all that has been committed to us by God the Creator. We have been reluctant followers of Jesus Christ in his mission to bring all persons into a community of love. Though called by the Holy Spirit to become new creatures in Christ, we have resisted the further call to become the people of God in our dealings with each other and the earth on which we live.

We affirm our unity in Jesus Christ while acknowledging differences in applying our faith in different cultural contexts as we live out the gospel. We stand united in declaring our faith that God's grace is available to all, that nothing can separate us from the love of God in Christ Jesus.

Grateful for God's forgiving love, in which we live and by which we are judged, and affirming our belief in the inestimable worth of each individual, we renew our commitment to become faithful witnesses to the gospel, not alone to the ends of earth, but also to the depths of our common life and work.

¶ 160.   I. THE NATURAL WORLD

All creation is the Lord's, and we are responsible for the ways in which we use and abuse it. Water, air, soil, minerals, energy resources, plants, animal life, and space are to be valued and conserved because they are God's creation and not solely because they are useful to human beings. God has granted us stewardship of creation. We should meet these stewardship duties through acts of loving care and respect. Economic, political, social, and technological developments have increased our human numbers, and lengthened and enriched our lives. However, these developments have led to regional defoliation, dramatic extinction of species, massive human suffering, overpopulation, and misuse and overconsumption of natural and nonrenewable resources, particularly by industrialized societies. This continued course of action jeopardizes the natural heritage that God has entrusted to all generations. Therefore, let us recognize the responsibility of the church and its members to place a high priority on changes in economic, political, social, and technological lifestyles to support a more ecologically equitable and sustainable world leading to a higher quality of life for all of God's creation.

A) *Water, Air, Soil, Minerals, Plants*—We support and encourage social policies that serve to reduce and control the creation of industrial byproducts and waste; facilitate the safe processing and disposal of toxic and nuclear waste and move toward the elimination of both; encourage reduction of municipal waste; provide for appropriate recycling and disposal of municipal waste; and assist the cleanup of polluted air, water, and soil. We call for the preservation of old-growth forests and other irreplaceable natural treasures, as well as preservation of endangered plant species. We support measures designed to maintain and restore natural ecosystems. We support policies that develop alternatives to chemicals used for growing, processing, and preserving food, and we strongly urge adequate research into their effects upon God's creation prior to utilization. We urge development of international agreements concerning equitable utilization of the world's resources for human benefit so long as the integrity of the earth is maintained. We are deeply concerned about the privatization of water resources, the bottling of water to be sold as a commodity for profit, and the resources that go into packaging bottled water. We urge all municipalities and other governmental organizations to develop processes for determining sustainability of water resources and to determine the environmental, economic, and social consequences of privatization of water resources prior to the licensing and approval thereof.

B) *Energy Resources Utilization*—The whole earth is God's good creation and as such has inherent value. We are aware that the current utilization of energy resources threatens this creation at its very foundation. As members of The United Methodist Church we are committed to approaching creation, energy production, and especially creation's resources in a responsible, careful and economic way. We call upon all to take measures to save energy. Everybody should adapt his or her lifestyle to the average consumption of energy that respects the limits of the planet earth. We encourage persons to limit CO_2 emissions toward the goal of one tonne per person annually. We strongly advocate for the priority of the development of renewable energies. The deposits of carbon, oil, and gas resources are limited and their continuous utilization accelerates global warming. The use of nuclear power is no solution for avoiding CO_2 emissions.

Nuclear power plants are vulnerable, unsafe, and potential health risks. A safe, permanent storage of nuclear waste cannot be guaranteed. It is therefore not responsible to future generations to operate them. The production of agricultural fuels and the use of biomass plants rank lower than the provision of safe food supplies and the continued existence for small farming businesses.

C) Animal Life—We support regulations that protect and conserve the life and health of animals, including those ensuring the humane treatment of pets, domesticated animals, animals used in research, wildlife, and the painless slaughtering of meat animals, fish, and fowl. We recognize unmanaged and managed commercial, multinational, and corporate exploitation of wildlife and the destruction of the ecosystems on which they depend threatens the balance of natural systems, compromises biodiversity, reduces resilience, and threatens ecosystem services. We encourage commitment to effective implementation of national and international governmental and business regulations and guidelines for the conservation of all animal species with particular support to safeguard those threatened with extinction.

D) Global Climate Stewardship—We acknowledge the global impact of humanity's disregard for God's creation. Rampant industrialization and the corresponding increase in the use of fossil fuels have led to a buildup of pollutants in the earth's atmosphere. These "greenhouse gas" emissions threaten to alter dramatically the earth's climate for generations to come with severe environmental, economic, and social implications. The adverse impacts of global climate change disproportionately affect individuals and nations least responsible for the emissions. We therefore support efforts of all governments to require mandatory reductions in greenhouse gas emissions and call on individuals, congregations, businesses, industries, and communities to reduce their emissions.

E) Space—The universe, known and unknown, is the creation of God and is due the respect we are called to give the earth. We therefore reject any nation's efforts to weaponized space and urge that all nations pursue the peaceful and collaborative development of space technologies and of outer space itself.

F) Science and Technology—We recognize science as a legitimate interpretation of God's natural world. We affirm the validity of the claims of science in describing the natural world and in determining what is scientific. We preclude science from making authoritative claims about theological issues and theology from making authoritative claims about scientific issues. We find that science's descriptions of cosmological, geological, and biological evolution are not in conflict with theology. We recognize medical, technical, and scientific technologies as legitimate uses of God's natural world when such use enhances human life and enables all of God's children to develop their God-given creative potential without violating our ethical convictions about the relationship of humanity to the natural world. We reexamine our ethical convictions as our understanding of the natural world increases. We find that as science expands human understanding of the natural world, our understanding of the mysteries of God's creation and word are enhanced.

In acknowledging the important roles of science and technology, however, we also believe that theological understandings of human experience are crucial to a full understanding of the place of humanity in the universe. Science and theology are complementary rather than mutually incompatible. We therefore encourage dialogue between the scientific and theological communities and seek the kind of participation that will enable humanity to sustain life on earth and, by God's grace, increase the quality of our common lives together.

G) Food Safety—We support policies that protect the food supply and that ensure the public's right to know the content of the foods they are eating. We call for rigorous inspections and controls on the biological safety of all foodstuffs intended for human consumption. We urge independent testing for chemical residues in food, and the removal from the market of foods contaminated with potentially hazardous levels of pesticides, herbicides, or fungicides; drug residues from animal antibiotics, steroids, or hormones; contaminants due to pollution that are carried by air, soil, or water from incinerator plants or other industrial operations. We call for clear labeling of all processed, genetically created, or genetically altered foods, with premarket safety testing required. We oppose weakening the standards for organic foods. We call for policies that encourage and support a gradual transition to sustainable and organic agriculture.

H) Food Justice—We support policies that increase access to quality food, particularly for those with the fewest resources. We affirm local, sustainable, and small-scale agriculture opportunities that allow communities to feed themselves. We decry policies that make food inaccessible to the communities where it is grown and the farmworkers involved in its growth.

¶ 161.   II. THE NURTURING COMMUNITY

The community provides the potential for nurturing human beings into the fullness of their humanity. We believe we have a responsibility to innovate, sponsor, and evaluate new forms of community that will encourage development of the fullest potential in individuals. Primary for us is the gospel understanding that all persons are important—because they are human beings created by God and loved through and by Jesus Christ and not because they have merited significance. We therefore support social climates in which human communities are maintained and strengthened for the sake of all persons and their growth. We also encourage all individuals to be sensitive to others by using appropriate language when referring to all persons. Language of a derogatory nature (with regard to race, nationality, ethnic background, gender, sexuality, and physical differences) does not reflect value for one another and contradicts the gospel of Jesus Christ.

A) Culture and Identity—We believe that our primary identity is as children of God. With that identity comes societal and cultural constructions that have both positive and negative impacts on humanity and the Church. Cultural identity evolves through our history, traditions, and experiences. The Church seeks to fully embrace and nurture cultural formation and competency as a means to be fully one body, expressed in multiple ways. Each of us has multiple identities of equal value that intersect to form our complete self. We affirm that no identity or culture has more legitimacy than any other. We call the Church to challenge any hierarchy of cultures or identities. Through relationships within and among cultures we are called to and have the responsibility for learning from each other, showing mutual respect for our differences and similarities as we experience the diversity of perspectives and viewpoints.

B) The Family—We believe the family to be the basic human community through which persons are nurtured and sustained in mutual love, responsibility, respect, and fidelity. We affirm the importance of loving parents for all children. We also understand the family as encompassing a wider range of options than that of the two-generational unit of parents and children (the nuclear family). We affirm shared responsibility for parenting where there are two parents and encourage social, economic, and religious efforts to maintain and strengthen relationships within families in order that every member may be assisted toward complete personhood.

C) Marriage—We affirm the sanctity of the marriage covenant that is expressed in love, mutual support, personal commitment, and shared fidelity between a man and a woman. We believe that God's blessing rests upon such marriage, whether or not there are children of the union. We reject social norms that assume different standards for women than for men in marriage. We support laws in civil society that define marriage as the union of one man and one woman.[2]

D) Divorce—God's plan is for lifelong, faithful marriage. The church must be on the forefront of premarital, marital, and postmarital counseling in order to create and preserve healthy relationships. However, when a married couple is estranged beyond reconciliation, even after thoughtful consideration and counsel, divorce is a regrettable alternative in the midst of brokenness. We grieve over the devastating emotional, spiritual, and economic consequences of divorce for all involved, understanding that women and especially children are disproportionately impacted by such burdens. As the Church we are concerned about high divorce rates. It is recommended that methods of mediation be used to minimize the adversarial nature and fault-finding that are often part of our current judicial processes, encouraging reconciliation wherever possible. We also support efforts by governments to reform divorce laws and other aspects of family law in order to address negative trends such as high divorce rates.

Although divorce publicly declares that a marriage no longer exists, other covenantal relationships resulting from the marriage remain, such as the nurture and support of children and extended family ties. We urge respectful negotiations in deciding the custody of minor children and support the consideration of either or both parents for this responsibility in that custody not be reduced to financial support, control, or manipulation and retaliation. The welfare of each child is the most important consideration.

Divorce does not preclude a new marriage. We encourage an intentional commitment of the Church and society to minister compassionately to those in the process of divorce, as well as members of divorced and remarried families, in a community of faith where God's grace is shared by all.

E) Single Persons—We affirm the integrity of single persons, and we reject all social practices that discriminate or social attitudes that are prejudicial against persons because they are single. This also includes single parents, and we recognize the extra responsibilities involved.

---

2. See Judicial Council Decision 694.

F) Women and Men—We affirm with Scripture the common humanity of male and female, both having equal worth in the eyes of God. We reject the erroneous notion that one gender is superior to another, that one gender must strive against another, and that members of one gender may receive love, power, and esteem only at the expense of another. We especially reject the idea that God made individuals as incomplete fragments, made whole only in union with another. We call upon women and men alike to share power and control, to learn to give freely and to receive freely, to be complete and to respect the wholeness of others. We seek for every individual opportunities and freedom to love and be loved, to seek and receive justice, and to practice ethical self-determination. We understand our gender diversity to be a gift from God, intended to add to the rich variety of human experience and perspective; and we guard against attitudes and traditions that would use this good gift to leave members of one sex more vulnerable in relationships than members of another.

G) Human Sexuality—We affirm that sexuality is God's good gift to all persons. We call everyone to responsible stewardship of this sacred gift.

Although all persons are sexual beings whether or not they are married, sexual relations are affirmed only with the covenant of monogamous, heterosexual marriage.

We deplore all forms of the commercialization, abuse, and exploitation of sex. We call for strict global enforcement of laws prohibiting the sexual exploitation of children and for adequate protection, guidance, and counseling for abused children. All persons, regardless of age, gender, marital status, or sexual orientation, are entitled to have their human and civil rights ensured and to be protected against violence. The Church should support the family in providing age-appropriate education regarding sexuality to children, youth, and adults.

We affirm that all persons are individuals of sacred worth, created in the image of God. All persons need the ministry of the Church in their struggles for human fulfillment, as well as the spiritual and emotional care of a fellowship that enables reconciling relationships with God, with others, and with self. The United Methodist Church does not condone the practice of homosexuality and considers this practice incompatible with Christian teaching. We affirm that God's grace is available to all. We will seek to live together in Christian community, welcoming, forgiving, and loving one another, as Christ has loved and accepted us. We implore families and churches not to reject or condemn lesbian and gay members and friends. We commit ourselves to be in ministry for and with all persons.[3]

H) Family Violence and Abuse—We recognize that family violence and abuse in all its forms—verbal, psychological, physical, sexual—is detrimental to the covenant of the human community. We encourage the Church to provide a safe environment, counsel, and support for the victim and to work with the abuser to understand the root causes and forms of abuse and to overcome such behaviors. Regardless of the cause or the abuse, both the victim and the abuser need the love of the Church. While we deplore the actions of the abuser, we affirm that person to be in need of God's redeeming love.

I) Sexual Abuse—Violent, disrespectful, or abusive sexual expressions do not confirm sexuality as God's good gift. We reject all sexual expressions that damage the humanity God has given us as birthright, and we affirm only that sexual expression that enhances that same humanity. We believe that sexual relations where one or both partners are exploitative, abusive, or promiscuous are beyond the parameters of acceptable Christian behavior and are ultimately destructive to individuals, families, and the social order. We deplore all forms of the commercialization and exploitation of sex, with their consequent cheapening and degradation of human personality. To lose freedom and be sold by someone else for sexual purposes is a form of slavery, and we denounce such business and support the abused and their right to freedom.

We call for strict global enforcement of laws prohibiting the sexual exploitation or use of children by adults and encourage efforts to hold perpetrators legally and financially responsible. We call for the establishment of adequate protective services, guidance, and counseling opportunities for children thus abused.

J) Sexual Harassment—We believe human sexuality is God's good gift. One abuse of this good gift is sexual harassment. We define sexual harassment as any unwanted sexual comment, advance, or demand, either verbal or physical, that is reasonably perceived by the recipient as demeaning, intimidating, or coercive. Sexual harassment must be understood as an exploitation of a power relationship rather than as an exclusively sexual issue. Sexual harassment includes, but is not limited to, the creation of a hostile or abusive working environment resulting from discrimination on the basis of

---

3. See Judicial Council Decision 702.

gender. Contrary to the nurturing community, sexual harassment creates improper, coercive, and abusive conditions wherever it occurs in society. Sexual harassment undermines the social goal of equal opportunity and the climate of mutual respect between men and women. Unwanted sexual attention is wrong and discriminatory. Sexual harassment interferes with the moral mission of the Church.

K) Abortion—The beginning of life and the ending of life are the God-given boundaries of human existence. While individuals have always had some degree of control over when they would die, they now have the awesome power to determine when and even whether new individuals will be born. Our belief in the sanctity of unborn human life makes us reluctant to approve abortion.

But we are equally bound to respect the sacredness of the life and well-being of the mother and the unborn child.

We recognize tragic conflicts of life with life that may justify abortion, and in such cases we support the legal option of abortion under proper medical procedures by certified medical providers. We support parental, guardian, or other responsible adult notification and consent before abortions can be performed on girls who have not yet reached the age of legal adulthood. We cannot affirm abortion as an acceptable means of birth control, and we unconditionally reject it as a means of gender selection or eugenics (see Resolution 3184).

We oppose the use of late-term abortion known as dilation and extraction (partial-birth abortion) and call for the end of this practice except when the physical life of the mother is in danger and no other medical procedure is available, or in the case of severe fetal anomalies incompatible with life. This procedure shall be performed only by certified medical providers. Before providing their services, abortion providers should be required to offer women the option of anesthesia.

We call all Christians to a searching and prayerful inquiry into the sorts of conditions that may cause them to consider abortion. We entrust God to provide guidance, wisdom, and discernment to those facing an unintended pregnancy.

The Church shall offer ministries to reduce unintended pregnancies. We commit our Church to continue to provide nurturing ministries to those who terminate a pregnancy, to those in the midst of a crisis pregnancy, and to those who give birth.

We mourn and are committed to promoting the diminishment of high abortion rates. The Church shall encourage ministries to reduce unintended pregnancies such as comprehensive, age-appropriate sexuality education, advocacy in regard to contraception, and support of initiatives that enhance the quality of life for all women and girls around the globe.

Young adult women disproportionately face situations in which they feel that they have no choice due to financial, educational, relational, or other circumstances beyond their control. The Church and its local congregations and campus ministries should be in the forefront of supporting existing ministries and developing new ministries that help such women in their communities. They should also support those crisis pregnancy centers and pregnancy resource centers that compassionately help women explore all options related to unplanned pregnancy. We particularly encourage the Church, the government, and social service agencies to support and facilitate the option of adoption. (See ¶ 161M.) We affirm and encourage the Church to assist the ministry of crisis pregnancy centers and pregnancy resource centers that compassionately help women find feasible alternatives to abortion.

Governmental laws and regulations do not provide all the guidance required by the informed Christian conscience. Therefore, a decision concerning abortion should be made only after thoughtful and prayerful consideration by the parties involved, with medical, family, pastoral, and other appropriate counsel.

L) Ministry With Those Who Have Experienced an Abortion—We urge local pastors to become informed about the symptoms and behaviors associated with post-abortion stress. We commit our Church to continue to provide nurturing ministries to those who terminate a pregnancy, to those in the midst of a crisis pregnancy, and to those who give birth. We further encourage local churches to make available contact information for counseling agencies that offer programs to address post-abortion stress for all seeking help.

M) Adoption—Children are a gift from God to be welcomed and received. We recognize that some circumstances of birth make the rearing of a child difficult. We affirm and support the birth parent(s) whose choice it is to allow the child to be adopted. We recognize the agony, strength, and courage of the birth parent(s) who choose(s) in hope, love, and prayer to offer the child for adoption. In addition, we also recognize the anxiety, strength, and courage of those who choose in hope, love, and prayer to be able to care for a child. We affirm and support the adoptive parent(s)' desire to rear an adopted child as they would a biological child. When circumstances warrant adoption, we support the use of proper legal procedures. When appropriate and possible, we encourage open adoption so that a child may know all information and people related to them, both medically and relationally. We support and encourage greater awareness and education to promote adoption of a wide variety of children through foster care, international adoption, and domestic adoption. We commend the birth parent(s), the receiving parent(s), and the child to the care of the Church, that grief might be shared, joy might be celebrated, and the child might be nurtured in a community of Christian love.

N) Faithful Care for Dying Persons—While we applaud medical science for efforts to prevent disease and illness and for advances in treatment that extend the meaningful life of human beings, we recognize that every mortal life will ultimately end in death. Death is never a sign that God has abandoned us, no matter what the circumstances of the death might be. As Christians we must always be prepared to surrender the gift of mortal life and claim the gift of eternal life through the death and resurrection of Jesus Christ. Care for dying persons is part of our stewardship of the divine gift of life when cure is no longer possible. We encourage the use of medical technologies to provide palliative care at the end of life when life-sustaining treatments no longer support the goals of life, and when they have reached their limits. There is no moral or religious obligation to use these when they impose undue burdens or only extend the process of dying. Dying persons and their families are free to discontinue treatments when they cease to be of benefit to the patient.

We recognize the agonizing personal and moral decisions faced by the dying, their physicians, their families, their friends, and their faith community. We urge that decisions faced by the dying be made with thoughtful and prayerful consideration by the parties involved, with medical, pastoral, and other appropriate counsel. We further urge that all persons discuss with their families, their physicians, and their pastoral counselors, their wishes for care at the end of life and provide advance directives for such care when they are not able to make these decisions for themselves. Even when one accepts the inevitability of death, the Church and society must continue to provide faithful care, including pain relief, companionship, support, and spiritual nurture for the dying person in the hard work of preparing for death. We encourage and support the concept of hospice care whenever possible at the end of life. Faithful care does not end at death but continues during bereavement as we care for grieving families. We reject euthanasia and any pressure upon the dying to end their lives. God has continued love and purpose for all persons, regardless of health. We affirm laws and policies that protect the rights and dignity of the dying.

O) Suicide—We believe that suicide is not the way a human life should end. Often suicide is the result of untreated depression, or untreated pain and suffering. The Church has an obligation to see that all persons have access to needed pastoral and medical care and therapy in those circumstances that lead to loss of self-worth, suicidal despair, and/or the desire to seek physician-assisted suicide. We encourage the Church to provide education to address the biblical, theological, social, and ethical issues related to death and dying, including suicide. United Methodist theological seminary courses should also focus on issues of death and dying, including suicide.

A Christian perspective on suicide begins with an affirmation of faith that nothing, including suicide, separates us from the love of God (Romans 8:38-39). Therefore, we deplore the condemnation of people who complete suicide, and we consider unjust the stigma that so often falls on surviving family and friends.

We encourage pastors and faith communities to address this issue through preaching and teaching. We urge pastors and faith communities to provide pastoral care to those at risk, survivors, and their families, and to those families who have lost loved ones to suicide, seeking always to remove the oppressive stigma around suicide. The Church opposes assisted suicide and euthanasia.

P) Sexual Assault—Sexual assault is wrong. We affirm the right of all people to live free from such assaults, encourage efforts of law enforcement to prosecute such crimes, and condemn rape in any form. It does not matter where the person is, what the person is wearing, whether or not he or she is intoxicated, if he or she is flirtatious, what is the victim's gender, or any other circumstance.

Q) Pornography—Scripture teaches that humans are created in God's image and that we are accountable to God through right relationship. Sexual images can celebrate the goodness of human sexuality through positive depiction in art, literature, and education. We deplore, however, images that distort this goodness and injure healthy sexual relationships.

We oppose all forms of pornography and consider its use a form of sexual misconduct. Pornography is sexually explicit material that portrays violence, abuse, coercion, domination, humiliation, or

degradation for the purpose of sexual arousal. Pornography sexually exploits and objectifies both women and men. Any sexually
explicit material that depicts children is abhorrent and victimizes
children. Pornography can ruin lives, careers, and relationships.

We grieve the pervasiveness of Internet pornography, including
among Christians, and especially its impact on young people and
marriages.

The Church is called to transformation and healing for all persons adversely affected by pornography. Congregations should
send a clear message of opposition to pornography and commitment to safe environments for everyone. We encourage strategies
to eradicate pornography, to support victims, and to provide open
and transparent conversation and education around sexuality and
sexual ethics. We also believe that people can be rehabilitated and
should have the opportunity to receive treatment; therefore, churches should seek ways to offer support and care for addressing issues of addiction. Further, all churches are encouraged to review
and update appropriate child, youth, and adult protection policies
to reflect The United Methodist Church's position that the use of
pornography is a form of sexual misconduct. By encouraging education, prevention, and pathways to recovery for all affected by
pornography, we live out our Wesleyan understanding of grace and
healing.

R) Bullying—Bullying is a growing problem in parts of the connection. It is a contributing factor in suicide and in the violence we
see in some cultures today. We affirm the right of all people, regardless of gender, socioeconomic status, race, religion, disability, age,
physical appearance, sexual orientation and gender identity, to be
free of unwanted aggressive behavior and harmful control tactics.

As the Church, we can play a pivotal role in ending this problem. We urge churches to seek opportunities to be trained in responding to the needs of those who have been bullied, to those who
perpetrate bullying, and to support those in authority who may witness or be called to intervene on behalf of those who have been bullied. Churches are urged to connect with community associations
and schools in this outreach.

We encourage churches to adopt a policy of zero tolerance for
bullying, including cyberbullying, within their spheres of influence; stand with persons being bullied; and take a leadership role in
working with the schools and community to prevent bullying.

¶ **162.** **III. THE SOCIAL COMMUNITY**

The rights and privileges a society bestows upon or withholds from those who comprise it indicate the relative esteem in which that society holds particular persons and groups of persons. We affirm all persons as equally valuable in the sight of God. We therefore work toward societies in which each person's value is recognized, maintained, and strengthened. We support the basic rights of all persons to equal access to housing, education, communication, employment, medical care, legal redress for grievances, and physical protection. We deplore acts of hate or violence against groups or persons based on race, color, national origin, ethnicity, age, gender, disability, status, economic condition, sexual orientation, gender identity, or religious affiliation. Our respect for the inherent dignity of all persons leads us to call for the recognition, protection, and implementation of the principles of *The Universal Declaration of Human Rights* so that communities and individuals may claim and enjoy their universal, indivisible, and inalienable rights.

A) Rights of Racial and Ethnic Persons—Racism is the combination of the power to dominate by one race over other races and a value system that assumes that the dominant race is innately superior to the others. Racism includes both personal and institutional racism. Personal racism is manifested through the individual expressions, attitudes, and/or behaviors that accept the assumptions of a racist value system and that maintain the benefits of this system. Institutional racism is the established social pattern that supports implicitly or explicitly the racist value system. Racism, manifested as sin, plagues and hinders our relationship with Christ, inasmuch as it is antithetical to the gospel itself. In many cultures white persons are granted unearned privileges and benefits that are denied to persons of color. We oppose the creation of a racial hierarchy in any culture. Racism breeds racial discrimination. We define racial discrimination as the disparate treatment and lack of full access and equity in resources, opportunities, and participation in the Church and in society based on race or ethnicity.

Therefore, we recognize racism as sin and affirm the ultimate and temporal worth of all persons. We rejoice in the gifts that particular ethnic histories and cultures bring to our total life. We commit as the Church to move beyond symbolic expressions and representative models that do not challenge unjust systems of power and access.

We commend and encourage the self-awareness of all racial and ethnic groups and oppressed people that leads them to demand their just and equal rights as members of society. We assert the obligation of society and people within the society to implement compensatory programs that redress long-standing, systemic social deprivation of racial and ethnic persons. We further assert the right of members of historically underrepresented racial and ethnic persons to equal and equitable opportunities in employment and promotion; to education and training of the highest quality; to nondiscrimination in voting, access to public accommodations, and housing purchase or rental; to credit, financial loans, venture capital, and insurance policies; to positions of leadership and power in all elements of our life together; and to full participation in the Church and society. We support affirmative action as one method of addressing the inequalities and discriminatory practices within the Church and society.

B) Rights of Religious Minorities—Religious persecution has been common in the history of civilization. We urge policies and practices that ensure the right of every religious group to exercise its faith free from legal, political, or economic restrictions. We condemn all overt and covert forms of religious intolerance, being especially sensitive to their expression in media stereotyping. We assert the right of all religions and their adherents to freedom from legal, economic, and social discrimination.

C) Rights of Children—Once considered the property of their parents, children are now acknowledged to be full human beings in their own right, but beings to whom adults and society in general have special obligations. Thus, we support the development of school systems and innovative methods of education designed to assist every child toward complete fulfillment as an individual person of worth. All children have the right to quality education, including full sex education appropriate to their stage of development that utilizes the best educational techniques and insights. Christian parents and guardians and the Church have the responsibility to ensure that children receive sex education consistent with Christian morality, including faithfulness in marriage and abstinence in singleness. Moreover, children have the rights to food, shelter, clothing, health care, and emotional well-being as do adults, and these rights we affirm as theirs regardless of actions or inactions of their parents or guardians. In particular, children must be protected from economic, physical, emotional, and sexual exploitation and abuse.

D) Rights of Young People—Our society is characterized by a large population of young people who frequently find full participation in society difficult. Therefore, we urge development of policies that encourage inclusion of young people in decision-making processes and that eliminate discrimination and exploitation. Creative and appropriate employment opportunities should be legally and socially available for young people.

E) Rights of the Aging—In a society that places primary emphasis upon youth, those growing old in years are frequently isolated from the mainstream of social existence. We support social policies that integrate the aging into the life of the total community, including sufficient incomes, increased and nondiscriminatory employment opportunities, educational and service opportunities, and adequate medical care and housing within existing communities. We urge social policies and programs, with emphasis on the unique concerns of older women and ethnic persons, that ensure to the aging the respect and dignity that is their right as senior members of the human community. Further, we urge increased consideration for adequate pension systems by employers, with provisions for the surviving spouse.

F) Rights of Women—We affirm women and men to be equal in every aspect of their common life. We therefore urge that every effort be made to eliminate sex-role stereotypes in activity and portrayal of family life and in all aspects of voluntary and compensatory participation in the Church and society. We affirm the right of women to equal treatment in employment, responsibility, promotion, and compensation. We affirm the importance of women in decision-making positions at all levels of Church and society and urge such bodies to guarantee their presence through policies of employment and recruitment. We support affirmative action as one method of addressing the inequalities and discriminatory practices within our Church and society. We urge employers of persons in dual career families, both in the Church and society, to apply proper consideration of both parties when relocation is considered. We affirm the right of women to live free from violence and abuse and urge governments to enact policies that protect women against all forms of violence and discrimination in any sector of society.

G) Rights of Men—Because we affirm women and men to be equal in every aspect of their common life, we also affirm the rights of men. We affirm equal opportunities in employment, responsibility, and promotion. Men should not be ignored or lose opportunities or influence because they are men.

We recognize that men are also victims of domestic violence and abuse. We encourage communities to offer the same policies and protection as provided for women in similar situations. We affirm the right of men to live free from violence and abuse and urge governments to enact policies that protect men against all forms of violence and discrimination in any sector of society.

We recognize that men's role in raising children is in equal importance to women's and call for equal rights as women in opportunities for parental leave. When parents divorce, men often have less contact with their children. We call for equal access to child-custody, but emphasize that the best interest of the child always is the most important.

H) Rights of Immigrants—We recognize, embrace, and affirm all persons, regardless of country of origin, as members of the family of God. We affirm the right of all persons to equal opportunities for employment, access to housing, health care, education, and freedom from social discrimination. We urge the Church and society to recognize the gifts, contributions, and struggles of those who are immigrants and to advocate for justice for all. We oppose immigration policies that separate family members from each other or that include detention of families with children, and we call on local churches to be in ministry with immigrant families.

I) Rights of Persons With Disabilities—We recognize and affirm the full humanity and personhood of all individuals with mental, physical, developmental, neurological, and psychological conditions or disabilities as full members of the family of God. We also affirm their rightful place in both the Church and society. We affirm the responsibility of the Church and society to be in ministry with children, youth, and adults with mental, physical, developmental, and/or psychological and neurological conditions or disabilities whose particular needs in the areas of mobility, communication, intellectual comprehension, or personal relationships might make more challenging their participation or that of their families in the life of the Church and the community. We urge the Church and society to recognize and receive the gifts of persons with disabilities to enable them to be full participants in the community of faith. We call the Church and society to be sensitive to, and advocate for, programs of rehabilitation, services, employment, education, appropriate housing, and transportation. We call on the Church and society to protect the civil rights of persons with all types and kinds of disabilities.

J) Equal Rights Regardless of Sexual Orientation—Certain basic human rights and civil liberties are due all persons. We are committed to supporting those rights and liberties for all persons, regardless of sexual orientation. We see a clear issue of simple justice in protecting the rightful claims where people have shared material resources, pensions, guardian relationships, mutual powers of attorney, and other such lawful claims typically attendant to contractual relationships that involve shared contributions, responsibilities, and liabilities, and equal protection before the law. Moreover, we support efforts to stop violence and other forms of coercion against all persons, regardless of sexual orientation.

K) Population—Since the growing worldwide population is increasingly straining the world's supply of food, minerals, and water and sharpening international tensions, the reduction of the rate of consumption of resources by the affluent and the reduction of current world population growth rates have become imperative. People have the duty to consider the impact on the total world community of their decisions regarding childbearing and should have access to information and appropriate means to limit their fertility, including voluntary sterilization. We affirm that programs to achieve a stabilized population should be placed in a context of total economic and social development, including an equitable use and control of resources; improvement in the status of women in all cultures; a human level of economic security, health care, and literacy for all. We oppose any policy of forced abortion or forced sterilization.

L) Alcohol and Other Drugs—We affirm our long-standing support of abstinence from alcohol as a faithful witness to God's liberating and redeeming love for persons. We support abstinence from the use of any illegal drugs. Since the use of illegal drugs, as well as illegal and problematic use of alcohol, is a major factor in crime, disease, death, and family dysfunction, we support educational programs as well as other prevention strategies encouraging abstinence from illegal drug use and, with regard to those who choose to consume alcoholic beverages, judicious use with deliberate and intentional restraint, with Scripture as a guide.

Millions of living human beings are testimony to the beneficial consequences of therapeutic drug use, and millions of others are testimony to the detrimental consequences of drug misuse. We encourage wise policies relating to the availability of potentially beneficial or potentially damaging prescription and over-the-counter drugs; we urge that complete information about their use and misuse be readily available to both doctor and patient. We support the strict administration of laws regulating the sale and distribution of alcohol and controlled substances. We support regulations that protect society from users of drugs of any kind, including alcohol, where it can be shown that a clear and present social danger exists. Drug-dependent persons and their family members, including those who are assessed or diagnosed as dependent on alcohol, are individuals of infinite human worth deserving of treatment, rehabilitation, and ongoing life-changing recovery. Misuse or abuse may also require intervention, in order to prevent progression into dependence. Because of the frequent interrelationship between alcohol abuse and mental illness, we call upon legislators and health care providers to make available appropriate mental illness treatment and rehabilitation for drug-dependent persons. We commit ourselves to assisting those who suffer from abuse or dependence, and their families, in finding freedom through Jesus Christ and in finding good opportunities for treatment, for ongoing counseling, and for reintegration into society.

M) Tobacco—We affirm our historic tradition of high standards of personal discipline and social responsibility. In light of the overwhelming evidence that tobacco smoking and the use of smokeless tobacco are hazardous to the health of persons of all ages, we recommend total abstinence from the use of tobacco. We urge that our educational and communication resources be utilized to support and encourage such abstinence. Further, we recognize the harmful effects of passive smoke and support the restriction of smoking in public areas and workplaces.

N) Medical Experimentation—Physical and mental health has been greatly enhanced through discoveries by medical science. It is imperative, however, that governments and the medical profession carefully enforce the requirements of the prevailing medical research standard, maintaining rigid controls in testing new technologies and drugs utilizing human beings. The standard requires that those engaged in research shall use human beings as research subjects only after obtaining full, rational, and uncoerced consent.

O) Genetic Technology—The responsibility of humankind to God's creation challenges us to deal carefully with and examine the possibilities of genetic research and technology in a conscientious, careful, and responsible way. We welcome the use of genetic technology for meeting fundamental human needs for health and a safe environment. We oppose the cloning of humans and the genetic manipulation of the gender of an unborn child.

Because of the effects of genetic technologies on all life, we call for effective guidelines and public accountability to safeguard against any action that might lead to abuse of these technologies, including political or military ends. We recognize that cautious, well-intended use of genetic technologies may sometimes lead to unanticipated harmful consequences. The risks of genetic technology that can hardly be calculated when breeding animals and plants and the negative ecological and social impacts on agriculture make the use of this technology doubtful. We approve modern methods of breeding that respect the existence of the natural borders of species.

Human gene therapies that produce changes that cannot be passed to offspring (somatic therapy) should be limited to the alleviation of suffering caused by disease. Genetic therapies for eugenic choices or that produce waste embryos are deplored. Genetic data of individuals and their families should be kept secret and held in strict confidence unless confidentiality is waived by the individual or by his or her family, or unless the collection and use of genetic identification data is supported by an appropriate court order. Because its long-term effects are uncertain, we oppose genetic therapy that results in changes that can be passed to offspring (germ-line therapy). All the genetic procedures must be accompanied by independent, ethically oriented measures of testing, approval, and control.

P) Rural Life—We support the right of persons and families to live and prosper as farmers, farm workers, merchants, professionals, and others outside of the cities and metropolitan centers. We believe our culture is impoverished and our people deprived of a meaningful way of life when rural and small-town living becomes difficult or impossible. We recognize that the improvement of this way of life may sometimes necessitate the use of some lands for nonagricultural purposes. We oppose the indiscriminate diversion of agricultural land for nonagricultural uses when nonagricultural land is available. Further, we encourage the preservation of appropriate lands for agriculture and open space uses through thoughtful land use programs. We support governmental and private programs designed to benefit the resident farmer rather than the factory farm and programs that encourage industry to locate in nonurban areas.

We further recognize that increased mobility and technology have brought a mixture of people, religions, and philosophies to rural communities that were once homogeneous. While often this is seen as a threat to or loss of community life, we understand it as an opportunity to uphold the biblical call to community for all persons. Therefore, we encourage rural communities and individuals to maintain a strong connection to the earth and to be open to: offering mutual belonging, caring, healing, and growth; sharing and celebrating cooperative leadership and diverse gifts; supporting mutual trust; and affirming individuals as unique persons of worth, and thus to practice shalom.

Q) Sustainable Agriculture—A prerequisite for meeting the nutritional needs of the world's population is an agricultural system that uses sustainable methods, respects ecosystems, and promotes a livelihood for people that work the land.

We support a sustainable agricultural system that will maintain and support the natural fertility of agricultural soil, promote the diversity of flora and fauna, and adapt to regional conditions and structures—a system where agricultural animals are treated humanely and where their living conditions are as close to natural systems as possible. We aspire to an effective agricultural system where plant, livestock, and poultry production maintains the natural ecological cycles, conserves energy, and reduces chemical input to a minimum.

Sustainable agriculture requires a global evaluation of the impact of agriculture on food and raw material production, the preservation of animal breeds and plant varieties, and the preservation and development of the cultivated landscape.

World trade of agricultural products needs to be based on fair trade and prices, based on the costs of sustainable production methods, and must consider the real costs of ecological damage. The needed technological and biological developments are those that support sustainability and consider ecological consequences.

R) Urban-Suburban Life—Urban-suburban living has become a dominant style of life for more and more persons. For many it furnishes economic, educational, social, and cultural opportunities. For others, it has brought alienation, poverty, and depersonalization. We in the Church have an opportunity and responsibility to help shape the future of urban-suburban life. Massive programs of renewal and social planning are needed to bring a greater degree of humanization into urban-suburban lifestyles. We must judge all programs, including economic and community development, new towns, and urban renewal, by the extent to which they protect and enhance human values, permit personal and political involvement, and make possible neighborhoods open to persons of all races, ages, and income levels. We affirm the efforts of all developers who place human values at the heart of their planning. We must help shape urban-suburban development so that it provides for the human need to identify with and find meaning in smaller social communities. At the same time, such smaller communities must be encouraged to assume responsibilities for the total urban-suburban community instead of isolating themselves from it.

S) Media Violence and Christian Values—In our society, the media plays an important role. It influences people all over the world. Content, representations, pictures, scenes, however, are often in a stark contrast to human and Christian values. We express disdain of dehumanizing portrayals, sensationalized through mass media "entertainment" and "news." These practices degrade humankind and violate the teachings of Christ and the Bible.

United Methodists, along with those of other faith groups, must be made aware that the mass media often undermine the truths of Christianity by promoting permissive lifestyles and detailing acts of graphic violence. Instead of encouraging, motivating, and inspiring its audiences to adopt lifestyles based on the sanctity of life, the entertainment industry often advocates the opposite, painting a cynical picture of violence, abuse, greed, profanity, and a constant denigration of the family. The media must be held accountable for the part they play in the decline of values we observe in society today. Many in the media remain aloof to the issue, claiming to reflect rather than to influence society. For the sake of our human family, Christians must work together to halt this erosion of moral and ethical values in the world community. We oppose any kind of sexist image as well as those that glorify violence. We reject the implicit message that conflicts can be resolved and just peace can be established by violence. Within the bounds of the freedom of speech and the freedom of the press, the media are responsible for respecting human rights. In support of these matters, we work together with all people of good will.

T) Information Communication Technology—Because effective personal communication is key to being a responsible and empowered member of society, and because of the power afforded by information communication technologies to shape society and enable individuals to participate more fully, we believe that access to these technologies is a basic right.

Information communication technologies provide us with information, entertainment, and a voice in society. They can be used to enhance our quality of life and provide us with a means to interact with each other, our government, and people and cultures all over the world. Most information about world events comes to us by broadcast, cable, print media, and the Internet. Concentrating the control of media to large commercial interests limits our choices and often provides a distorted view of human values. Therefore, we support the regulation of media communication technologies to ensure a variety of independent information sources and provide for the public good.

Personal communication technologies such as the Internet allow persons to communicate with each other and access vast information resources that can have commercial, cultural, political, and personal value. While the Internet can be used to nurture minds and spirits of children and adults, it is in danger of being overrun with commercial interests and is used by some to distribute inappropriate and illegal material. Therefore, the Internet must be managed responsibly in order to maximize its benefits while minimizing its risks, especially for children. Denying access in today's world to basic information communication technologies like the Internet due to their cost or availability, limits people's participation in their government and society. We support the goal of universal access to telephone and Internet services at an affordable price.

U) Persons Living With HIV and AIDS—Persons diagnosed as positive for Human Immune Virus (HIV) and with Acquired Immune Deficiency Syndrome (AIDS) often face rejection from their families and friends and various communities in which they work and interact. In addition, they are often faced with a lack of adequate health care, especially toward the end of life.

All individuals living with HIV and AIDS should be treated with dignity and respect.

We affirm the responsibility of the Church to minister to and with these individuals and their families regardless of how the disease was contracted. We support their rights to employment, appropriate medical care, full participation in public education, and full participation in the Church.

We urge the Church to be actively involved in the prevention of the spread of AIDS by providing educational opportunities to the congregation and the community. The Church should be available to provide counseling to the affected individuals and their families.

V) Right to Health Care—Health is a condition of physical, mental, social, and spiritual well-being. John 10:10b says, "I came so that they could have life—indeed, so that they could live life to the fullest." Stewardship of health is the responsibility of each person to whom health has been entrusted. Creating the personal, environmental, and social conditions in which health can thrive is a joint responsibility—public and private. We encourage individuals to pursue a healthy lifestyle and affirm the importance of preventive health care, health education, environmental and occupational safety, good nutrition, and secure housing in achieving health. Health care is a basic human right.

Providing the care needed to maintain health, prevent disease, and restore health after injury or illness is a responsibility each person owes others and government owes to all, a responsibility government ignores at its peril. In Ezekiel 34:4a, God points out the failures of the leadership of Israel to care for the weak: "You don't strengthen the weak, heal the sick, bind up the injured, bring back the strays, or seek out the lost." As a result all suffer. Like police and fire protection, health care is best funded through the government's ability to tax each person equitably and directly fund the provider entities. Countries facing a public health crisis such as HIV/AIDS must have access to generic medicines and to patented medicines. We affirm the right of men and women to have access to comprehensive reproductive health/family planning information and services that will serve as a means to prevent unplanned pregnancies, reduce abortions, and prevent the spread of HIV/AIDS. The right to health care includes care for persons with brain diseases, neurological conditions, or physical disabilities, who must be afforded the same access to health care as all other persons in our communities. It is unjust to construct or perpetuate barriers to physical or mental wholeness or full participation in community.

We believe it is a governmental responsibility to provide all citizens with health care.

We encourage hospitals, physicians, and medical clinics to provide access to primary health care to all people regardless of their health-care coverage or ability to pay for treatment.

W) Organ Transplantation and Donation—We believe that organ transplantation and organ donation are acts of charity, *agape* love, and self-sacrifice. We recognize the life-giving benefits of organ and other tissue donation and encourage all people of faith to become organ and tissue donors as a part of their love and ministry to others in need. We urge that it be done in an environment of respect for deceased and living donors and for the benefit of the recipients, and following protocols that carefully prevent abuse to donors and their families.

X) Mental Health—The World Health Organization defines mental health as "a state of well-being in which the individual realizes his or her own abilities, can cope with the normal stresses of life, can work productively and fruitfully, and is able to make a contribution to his or her community." Unfortunately, mental health eludes many in our world resulting in considerable distress, stigma, and isolation. Mental illness troubles our relationships because it can affect the way we process information, relate to others, and choose actions. Consequently, mental illnesses often are feared in ways that other illnesses are not. Nevertheless, we know that regardless of our illness we remain created in the image of God (Genesis 1:27) and that nothing can separate us from the love of God (Romans 8:38-39).

No person deserves to be stigmatized because of mental illness. Those with mental illness are no more violent than other persons are. Rather, they are much more likely to be victims of violence or preyed on by others. When stigma happens within the church, mentally ill persons and their families are further victimized. Persons with mental illness and their families have a right to be treated with respect on the basis of common humanity and accurate information. They also have a right and responsibility to obtain care appropriate to their condition. The United Methodist Church pledges to foster policies that promote compassion, advocate for access to care, and eradicate stigma within the Church and in communities.

¶ 163.   IV. THE ECONOMIC COMMUNITY

We claim all economic systems to be under the judgment of God no less than other facets of the created order. Therefore, we recognize the responsibility of governments to develop and implement sound fiscal and monetary policies that provide for the economic life of individuals and corporate entities and that ensure full employment and adequate incomes with a minimum of inflation. We believe private and public economic enterprises are responsible for the social costs of doing business, such as employment and environmental pollution, and that they should be held accountable for these costs. We support measures that would reduce the concentration of wealth in the hands of a few. We further support efforts to revise tax structures and to eliminate governmental support programs that now benefit the wealthy at the expense of other persons.

A) Property—We believe private ownership of property is a trusteeship under God, both in those societies where it is encouraged and where it is discouraged, but is limited by the overriding needs of society. We believe that Christian faith denies to any person or group of persons exclusive and arbitrary control of any other part of the created universe. Socially and culturally conditioned ownership of property is, therefore, to be considered a responsibility to God. We believe, therefore, governments have the responsibility, in the pursuit of justice and order under law, to provide procedures that protect the rights of the whole society as well as those of private ownership.

B) Collective Bargaining—We support the right of all public and private employees and employers to organize for collective bargaining into unions and other groups of their own choosing. Further, we support the right of both parties to protection in so doing and their responsibility to bargain in good faith within the framework of the public interest. In order that the rights of all members of the society may be maintained and promoted, we support innovative bargaining procedures that include representatives of the public interest in negotiation and settlement of labor-management contracts, including some that may lead to forms of judicial resolution of issues. We reject the use of violence by either party during collective bargaining or any labor/management disagreement. We likewise reject the permanent replacement of a worker who engages in a lawful strike.

C) Work and Leisure—Every person has the right to a job at a living wage. Where the private sector cannot or does not provide jobs for all who seek and need them, it is the responsibility of government to provide for the creation of such jobs. We support social measures that ensure the physical and mental safety of workers, that provide for the equitable division of products and services, and that encourage an increasing freedom in the way individuals may use their leisure time. We recognize the opportunity leisure provides for creative contributions to society and encourage methods that allow workers additional blocks of discretionary time. We support educational, cultural, and recreational outlets that enhance the use of such time. We believe that persons come before profits. We deplore the selfish spirit that often pervades our economic life. We support policies that encourage the sharing of ideas in the workplace, cooperative and collective work arrangements. We support rights of workers to refuse to work in situations that endanger health and/or life without jeopardy to their jobs. We support policies that would reverse the increasing concentration of business and industry into monopolies.

D) Consumption—Consumers should exercise their economic power to encourage the manufacture of goods that are necessary and beneficial to humanity while avoiding the desecration of the environment in either production or consumption. Consumers should avoid purchasing products made in conditions where workers are being exploited because of their age, gender, or economic status.

And while the limited options available to consumers make this extremely difficult to accomplish, buying "Fair Trade Certified" products is one sure way consumers can use their purchasing power to make a contribution to the common good. The International Standards of Fair Trade are based on ensuring livable wages for small farmers and their families, working with democratically run farming cooperatives, buying direct so that the benefits and profits from trade actually reach the farmers and their communities, providing vitally important advance credit, and encouraging ecologically sustainable farming practices. Consumers should not only seek out companies whose product lines reflect a strong commitment to these standards, but should also encourage expanded corporate participation in the Fair Trade market.

Consumers should evaluate their consumption of goods and services in the light of the need for enhanced quality of life rather than unlimited production of material goods. We call upon consumers, including local congregations and Church-related institutions, to organize to achieve these goals and to express dissatisfaction with harmful economic, social, or ecological practices through such appropriate methods as boycott, letter writing, corporate resolution, and advertisement.

E) Poverty—In spite of general affluence in the industrialized nations, the majority of persons in the world live in poverty. In order to provide basic needs such as food, clothing, shelter, education, health care, and other necessities, ways must be found to share more equitably the resources of the world. Increasing technology, when accompanied by exploitative economic practices, impoverishes many persons and makes poverty self-perpetuating. Poverty due to natural catastrophes and environmental changes is growing and needs attention and support. Conflicts and war impoverish the population on all sides, and an important way to support the poor will be to work for peaceful solutions.

As a church, we are called to support the poor and challenge the rich. To begin to alleviate poverty, we support such policies as: adequate income maintenance, quality education, decent housing, job training, meaningful employment opportunities, adequate medical and hospital care, humanization and radical revisions of welfare programs, work for peace in conflict areas and efforts to protect creation's integrity. Since low wages are often a cause of poverty, employers should pay their employees a wage that does not require them to depend upon government subsidies such as food stamps or welfare for their livelihood.

Because we recognize that the long-term reduction of poverty must move beyond services to and employment for the poor, which can be taken away, we emphasize measures that build and maintain the wealth of poor people, including asset-building strategies such as individual development savings accounts, micro-enterprise development programs, progams enabling home ownership, and financial management training and counseling. We call upon churches to develop these and other ministries that promote asset-building among the poor. We are especially mindful of the Global South, where investment and micro-enterprise are especially needed. We urge support for policies that will encourage equitable economic growth in the Global South and around the world, providing a just opportunity for all.

Poverty most often has systemic causes, and therefore we do not hold poor people morally responsible for their economic state.

F) Foreign Workers—For centuries people have moved across borders in search of work. In our global world this is still a relevant and increasing form of immigration. Improved wages, better working conditions, and jobs available are reasons for immigration due to work opportunities. Workers from other countries are in many societies an important resource to fill the society's need of workers. But foreign workers too often meet exploitation, absence of protecting laws, and unreasonable wages and working conditions.

We call upon governments and all employers to ensure for foreign workers the same economic, educational, and social benefits enjoyed by other citizens.

Foreign workers also need a religious fellowship, and we call for the churches to include these in their care and fellowships and to support them in their efforts for better conditions.

G) Gambling—Gambling is a menace to society, deadly to the best interests of moral, social, economic, and spiritual life, destructive of good government and good stewardship. As an act of faith and concern, Christians should abstain from gambling and should strive to minister to those victimized by the practice. Where gambling has become addictive, the Church will encourage such individuals to receive therapeutic assistance so that the individual's energies may be redirected into positive and constructive ends. The Church acknowledges the dichotomy that can occur when opposing gambling while supporting American Indian tribal sovereignty and self-determination. Therefore, the Church's role is to create sacred space to allow for dialogue and education that will promote a holistic understanding of the American Indians' historic quest for survival. The Church's prophetic call is to promote standards of justice and advocacy that would make it unnecessary and undesirable to resort to commercial gambling—including public lotteries, casinos, raffles, Internet gambling, gambling with an emerging wireless technology, and other games of chance—as a recreation, as an escape, or as a means of producing public revenue or funds for support of charities or government.

H) Family Farms—The value of family farms has long been affirmed as a significant foundation for free and democratic societies. In recent years, the survival of independent farmers worldwide has been threatened by various factors, including the increasing concentration of all phases of agriculture into the hands of a limited number of transnational corporations. The concentration of the food supply for the many into the hands of the few raises global questions of justice that cry out for vigilance and action.

We call upon the agribusiness sector to conduct itself with respect for human rights primarily in the responsible stewardship of daily bread for the world, and secondarily in responsible corporate citizenship that respects the rights of all farmers, small and large, to receive a fair return for honest labor. We advocate for the rights of people to possess property and to earn a living by tilling the soil.

We call upon governments to revise support programs that disproportionately benefit wealthier agricultural producers, so that more support can be given to programs that benefit medium- and smaller-sized farming operations, including programs that build rural processing, storage, distribution, and other agricultural infrastructure; which link local farmers to local schools; and which promote other community food security measures.

We call upon our churches to do all in their power to speak prophetically to the matters of food supply and the people who grow the food for the world and to develop ministries that build food security in local communities.

I) Corporate Responsibility—Corporations are responsible not only to their stockholders, but also to other stakeholders: their workers, suppliers, vendors, customers, the communities in which they do business, and for the earth, which supports them. We support the public's right to know what impact corporations have in these various arenas, so that people can make informed choices about which corporations to support.

We applaud corporations that voluntarily comply with standards that promote human well-being and protect the environment.

J) Finance—Financial institutions serve a vital role in society. They must guard, however, against abusive and deceptive lending practices that take advantage of the neediest among us for the gain of the richest. Banking regulations must prevent the collection of usurious interest that keeps people in cycles of debt. Personal-credit-issuing institutions must operate with responsibility and clarity that allow all parties to understand the full terms of agreements.

K) Trade and Investment—We affirm the importance of international trade and investment in an interdependent world. Trade and investment should be based on rules that support the dignity of the human person, a clean environment and our common humanity. Trade agreements must include mechanisms to enforce labor rights and human rights as well as environmental standards. Broad-based citizen advocacy and participation in trade negotiations must be ensured through democratic mechanisms of consultation and participation.

L) Graft and Corruption—God's good creation, the fullness of its bounty, and the loving, nurturing relationships that bind all together are intended by God to be enjoyed in freedom and responsible stewardship. To revere God's creation is a sacred trust that enables us to fashion just, equitable, sustainable relationships and communities. The strength, stability, security, and progress of such relationships and communities depend on the integrity of their social, economic, political, and cultural processes, institutions, and stakeholders. Graft, referring to unfair or illegal means of acquiring money, gain, or advantage, especially by abusing one's position in politics, business, and social institutions, transgresses human dignity and violates human rights. Corruption, referring to dishonest and undue exploitation of power for personal gain, subverts God's intention for the fullness of life and creation. Graft and corruption tangle the social thread of communities, erode the moral fiber of human relationships, and sully the reputation of social institutions. Legislative and judicial mechanisms, including a strong, just criminal justice system, must deal with graft and corruption at every level of society. Good, just political governance characterized by transparency, accountability, and integrity is crucial to the eradication of graft and corruption. Societies that are graft-ridden and plagued with corruption are needful of God's pardoning love and redeeming grace.

M) Public Indebtedness—The huge budget deficits produced by years of overspending by governments around the world is of great concern. We acknowledge that for a limited time in a nation's history governmental deficits are sometimes necessary. However, long periods of excessive overspending by governments have produced huge deficits and significant economic challenges for many nations. Such wanton carelessness cannot continue. Therefore, we call upon all governments to reduce budget deficits and to live within their means. We ask the governments and institutions that lend money to reduce significantly the interest rates on the money borrowed. We ask that public officials, when making financial adjustments, remember first and foremost obligations that promote the well-being of society such as the funding of schools and other opportunities that foster the growth of the individual, as well as agencies that care for the poor, the elderly, the disabled, and the disenfranchised.

We recognize that, if deficits are not brought under control, future generations will be shackled with a burden of public indebtedness that will force societies to live under the specter of coerced repayments, rising inflation, mass unemployment, and despair. Thus, this is not just a financial issue, but an issue of justice for those who are yet to be born. Wise stewardship is needed today to provide for future generations. We call on church leadership throughout the connection to encourage public officials to reduce public indebtedness and to begin the process toward balanced and fair budgets.

¶ 164.   V. THE POLITICAL COMMUNITY

While our allegiance to God takes precedence over our allegiance to any state, we acknowledge the vital function of government as a principal vehicle for the ordering of society. Because we know ourselves to be responsible to God for social and political life, we declare the following relative to governments:

A) Basic Freedoms and Human Rights—We hold governments responsible for the protection of the rights of the people to free and fair elections and to the freedoms of speech, religion, assembly, communications media, and petition for redress of grievances without fear of reprisal; to the right to privacy; and to the guarantee of the rights to adequate food, clothing, shelter, education, and health care. Blockades and embargoes that seek to impede the flow or free commerce of food and medicines are practices that cause pain and suffering, malnutrition, or starvation with all its detrimental consequences to innocent and noncombatant civilian populations, especially children. We reject these as instruments of domestic and foreign policy regardless of political or ideological views. The form and the leaders of all governments should be determined by exercise of the right to vote guaranteed to all adult citizens. We also strongly reject domestic surveillance and intimidation of political opponents by governments in power and all other misuses of elective or appointive offices. The use of detention and imprisonment for the harassment and elimination of political opponents or other dissidents violates fundamental human rights. Furthermore, the mistreatment or torture, and other cruel, inhumane, and degrading treatment or punishment of persons by governments for any purpose violates Christian teaching and must be condemned and/or opposed by Christians and churches wherever and whenever it occurs.

The Church regards the institution of slavery, the practice and commission of genocide, war crimes, crimes against humanity, and aggression as infamous and atrocious evils. Such evils are destructive of humanity, promote impunity, and therefore must be unconditionally prohibited by all governments and shall never be tolerated by the Church.

B) Political Responsibility—The strength of a political system depends upon the full and willing participation of its citizens. The church should continually exert a strong ethical influence upon the state, supporting policies and programs deemed to be just and opposing policies and programs that are unjust.

C) Church and State Relations—The United Methodist Church has for many years supported the separation of church and state. In some parts of the world this separation has guaranteed the diversity of religious expressions and the freedom to worship God according to each person's conscience. Separation of church and state means no organic union of the two, but it does permit interaction. The state should not use its authority to promote particular religious beliefs (including atheism), nor should it require prayer or worship in the public schools, but it should leave students free to practice their own religious convictions. We believe that the state should not attempt to control the church, nor should the church seek to dominate the state. The rightful and vital separation of church and state, which has served the cause of religious liberty, should not be misconstrued as the abolition of all religious expression from public life.

D) Freedom of Information—Citizens of all countries should have access to all essential information regarding their government and its policies. Illegal and unconscionable activities directed against persons or groups by their own governments must not be justified or kept secret, even under the guise of national security.

E) Education—We believe that every person has the right to education. We also believe that the responsibility for education of the young rests with the family, faith communities, and the government. In society, this function can best be fulfilled through public policies that ensure access for all persons to free public elementary and secondary schools and to post-secondary schools of their choice. Persons should not be precluded by financial barriers from access to church-related and other independent institutions of higher education. We affirm the right of public and independent colleges and universities to exist, and we endorse public policies that ensure access and choice and that do not create unconstitutional entanglements between church and state. We believe that colleges and universities are to ensure that academic freedom is protected for all members of the academic community and a learning environment is fostered that allows for a free exchange of ideas. We affirm the joining of reason and faith; therefore, we urge colleges and universities to guard the expression of religious life on campus.

F) Civil Obedience and Civil Disobedience—Governments and laws should be servants of God and of human beings. Citizens have a duty to abide by laws duly adopted by orderly and just process of government. But governments, no less than individuals, are subject to the judgment of God. Therefore, we recognize the right of individuals to dissent when acting under the constraint of conscience and, after having exhausted all legal recourse, to resist or disobey laws that they deem to be unjust or that are discriminately enforced. Even then, respect for law should be shown by refraining from violence and by being willing to accept the costs of disobedience. We do not encourage or condone any form of violent protest as a legitimate exercise of free speech or civil disobedience. We offer our prayers for those in rightful authority who serve the public, and we support their efforts to afford justice and equal opportunity for all people. We assert the duty of churches to support those who suffer because of their stands of conscience represented by nonviolent beliefs or acts. We urge governments to ensure civil rights, as defined by the International Covenant on Civil and Political Rights, to persons in legal jeopardy because of those nonviolent acts.

G) The Death Penalty—We believe the death penalty denies the power of Christ to redeem, restore, and transform all human beings. The United Methodist Church is deeply concerned about crime throughout the world and the value of any life taken by a murder or homicide. We believe all human life is sacred and created by God and therefore, we must see all human life as significant and valuable. When governments implement the death penalty (capital punishment), then the life of the convicted person is devalued and all possibility of change in that person's life ends. We believe in the resurrection of Jesus Christ and that the possibility of reconciliation with Christ comes through repentance. This gift of reconciliation is offered to all individuals without exception and gives all life new dignity and sacredness. For this reason, we oppose the death penalty (capital punishment) and urge its elimination from all criminal codes.

H) Criminal and Restorative Justice—To protect all persons from encroachment upon their personal and property rights, governments have established mechanisms of law enforcement and courts. A wide array of sentencing options serves to express community outrage, incapacitate dangerous offenders, deter crime, and offer opportunities for rehabilitation. We support governmental measures designed to reduce and eliminate crime that are consistent with respect for the basic freedom of persons.

We reject all misuse of these mechanisms, including their use for the purpose of revenge or for persecuting or intimidating those whose race, appearance, lifestyle, economic condition, or beliefs differ from those in authority. We reject all careless, callous, or discriminatory enforcement of law that withholds justice from persons with disabilities and all those who do not speak the language of the country in which they are in contact with the law enforcement. We further support measures designed to remove the social conditions that lead to crime, and we encourage continued positive interaction between law enforcement officials and members of the community at large.

In the love of Christ, who came to save those who are lost and vulnerable, we urge the creation of a genuinely new system for the care and restoration of victims, offenders, criminal justice officials, and the community as a whole. Restorative justice grows out of biblical authority, which emphasizes a right relationship with God, self, and community. When such relationships are violated or broken through crime, opportunities are created to make things right.

Most criminal justice systems around the world are retributive. These retributive justice systems profess to hold the offender accountable to the state and use punishment as the equalizing tool for accountability. In contrast, restorative justice seeks to hold the offender accountable to the victimized person, and to the disrupted community. Through God's transforming power, restorative justice seeks to repair the damage, right the wrong, and bring healing to all involved, including the victim, the offender, the families, and the community. The Church is transformed when it responds to the claims of discipleship by becoming an agent of healing and systemic change.

I) Military Service—We deplore war and urge the peaceful settlement of all disputes among nations. From the beginning, the Christian conscience has struggled with the harsh realities of violence and war, for these evils clearly frustrate God's loving purposes for humankind. We yearn for the day when there will be no more war and people will live together in peace and justice. Some of us believe that war, and other acts of violence, are never acceptable to Christians. We also acknowledge that many Christians believe that, when peaceful alternatives have failed, the force of arms may regretfully be preferable to unchecked aggression, tyranny, and genocide. We honor the witness of pacifists who will not allow us to become complacent about war and violence. We also respect those who support the use of force, but only in extreme situations and only when the need is clear beyond reasonable doubt, and through appropriate international organizations. We urge the establishment of the rule of law in international affairs as a means of elimination of war, violence, and coercion in these affairs.

We reject national policies of enforced military service as incompatible with the gospel. We acknowledge the agonizing tension created by the demand for military service by national governments. We urge all young adults to seek the counsel of the Church as they reach a conscientious decision concerning the nature of their responsibility as citizens. Pastors are called upon to be available for counseling with all young adults who face conscription or who are considering voluntary enlistment in the armed forces, including those who conscientiously refuse to cooperate with a system of conscription.

We support and extend the ministry of the Church to those persons who conscientiously oppose all war, or any particular war, and who therefore refuse to serve in the armed forces or to cooperate with systems of military conscription. We also support and extend the Church's ministry to all persons. This includes those who conscientiously choose to serve in the armed forces or to accept alternative service. When persons choose to serve in the armed forces, we support their right to adequate care for injuries suffered, and advocate for sufficient resources to meet their physical and mental health needs, both during and after their service. We are aware that we can become guilty both by military action and by conscientious objection, and that we all are dependent on God's forgiveness.

¶ 165.   VI. THE WORLD COMMUNITY

God's world is one world. The unity now being thrust upon us by technological revolution has far outrun our moral and spiritual capacity to achieve a stable world. The enforced unity of humanity, increasingly evident on all levels of life, presents the Church as well as all people with problems that will not wait for answers: injustice, war, exploitation, privilege, population, international ecological crisis, proliferation of arsenals of nuclear weapons, development of transnational business organizations that operate beyond the effective control of any governmental structure, and the increase of tyranny in all its forms. This generation must find viable answers to these and related questions if humanity is to continue on this earth. We commit ourselves as a Church to the achievement of a world community that is a fellowship of persons who honestly love one another. We pledge ourselves to seek the meaning of the gospel in all issues that divide people and threaten the growth of world community.

A) Nations and Cultures—As individuals are affirmed by God in their diversity, so are nations and cultures. We recognize that no nation or culture is absolutely just and right in its treatment of its own people, nor is any nation totally without regard for the welfare of its citizens. The Church must regard nations as accountable for unjust treatment of their citizens and others living within their borders. While recognizing valid differences in culture and political philosophy, we stand for justice and peace in every nation.

B) National Power and Responsibility—Some nations possess more military and economic power than do others. Upon the powerful rests responsibility to exercise their wealth and influence with restraint. We will promote restorative justice strategies to support positive social change and peace building. We affirm the right and duty of people of all nations to determine their own destiny. We urge the major political powers to use their nonviolent power to maximize the political, social, and economic self-determination of other nations rather than to further their own special interests. We applaud international efforts to develop a more just international economic order in which the limited resources of the earth will be used to the maximum benefit of all nations and peoples. We urge Christians in every society to encourage the governments under which they live and the economic entities within their societies to aid and work for the development of more just economic orders.

C) War and Peace—We believe war is incompatible with the teachings and example of Christ. We therefore reject war as an instrument of national foreign policy. We oppose unilateral first/preemptive strike actions and strategies on the part of any government. As disciples of Christ, we are called to love our enemies, seek justice, and serve as reconcilers of conflict. We insist that the first moral duty of all nations is to work together to resolve by peaceful means every dispute that arises between or among them. We advocate the extension and strengthening of international treaties and institutions that provide a framework within the rule of law for responding to aggression, terrorism, and genocide. We believe that human values must outweigh military claims as governments determine their priorities; that the militarization of society must be challenged and stopped; that the manufacture, sale, and deployment of armaments must be reduced and controlled; and that the production, possession, or use of nuclear weapons be condemned. Consequently, we endorse general and complete disarmament under strict and effective international control.

D) Justice and Law—Persons and groups must feel secure in their life and right to live within a society if order is to be achieved and maintained by law. We denounce as immoral an ordering of life that perpetuates injustice and impedes the pursuit of peace. Peoples and nations feel secure in the world community when law, order, and human rights are respected and upheld.

Believing that international justice requires the participation of all peoples and nations, we endorse the United Nations, its related bodies, the International Court of Justice, and the International Criminal Court as the best instruments now in existence to achieve a world of justice and law. We commend the efforts of all people in all countries who pursue world peace through law. We endorse international aid and cooperation on all matters of need and conflict. We urge acceptance for membership in the United Nations of all nations who wish such membership and who accept United Nations responsibility. We urge the United Nations to take a more aggressive role in the development of international arbitration of disputes and actual conflicts among nations by developing binding third-party arbitration. Bilateral or multilateral efforts outside of the United Nations should work in concert with, and not contrary to, its purposes. We reaffirm our historic concern for the world as our parish and seek for all persons and peoples full and equal membership in a truly world community.

¶ 166.   VII. OUR SOCIAL CREED

We believe in God, Creator of the world; and in Jesus Christ, the Redeemer of creation. We believe in the Holy Spirit, through whom we acknowledge God's gifts, and we repent of our sin in misusing these gifts to idolatrous ends.

We affirm the natural world as God's handiwork and dedicate ourselves to its preservation, enhancement, and faithful use by humankind.

We joyfully receive for ourselves and others the blessings of community, sexuality, marriage, and the family.

We commit ourselves to the rights of men, women, children, youth, young adults, the aging, and people with disabilities; to improvement of the quality of life; and to the rights and dignity of all persons.

We believe in the right and duty of persons to work for the glory of God and the good of themselves and others and in the protection of their welfare in so doing; in the rights to property as a trust from God, collective bargaining, and responsible consumption; and in the elimination of economic and social distress.

We dedicate ourselves to peace throughout the world, to the rule of justice and law among nations, and to individual freedom for all people of the world.

We believe in the present and final triumph of God's Word in human affairs and gladly accept our commission to manifest the life of the gospel in the world. Amen.

(It is recommended that this statement of Social Principles be continually available to United Methodist Christians and that it be emphasized regularly in every congregation. It is further recommended that "Our Social Creed" be frequently used in Sunday worship.)

A COMPANION LITANY TO OUR SOCIAL CREED

God in the Spirit revealed in Jesus Christ,
calls us by grace
> *to be renewed in the image of our Creator,*
> *that we may be one*
> *in divine love for the world.*

Today is the day
God cares for the integrity of creation,
> wills the healing and wholeness of all life,
> weeps at the plunder of earth's goodness.

And so shall we.

Today is the day
God embraces all hues of humanity,
> delights in diversity and difference,
> favors solidarity transforming strangers into friends.

And so shall we.

Today is the day
God cries with the masses of starving people,
> despises growing disparity between rich and poor,
> demands justice for workers in the marketplace.

And so shall we.

Today is the day
God deplores violence in our homes and streets,
> rebukes the world's warring madness,
> humbles the powerful and lifts up the lowly.

And so shall we.

Today is the day
God calls for nations and peoples to live in peace,
> celebrates where justice and mercy embrace,
> exults when the wolf grazes with the lamb.

And so shall we.

Today is the day
God brings good news to the poor,
> *proclaims release to the captives,*
> *gives sight to the blind, and*
> *sets the oppressed free.*
And so shall we.

Teaching
the Social Principles

The Social Principles cover a lot of controversial ground. Some of us are comfortable discussing the Social Principles, and others of us may steer clear of the conflicts and so avoid discussing controversial issues altogether. This avoidance proves in the end to be a counterproductive (and ultimately unhealthy) practice. Respectful conversation, even when we disagree, actually carries the potential to bring us closer to each other as a diverse community. Living out the Social Principles need not always imply agreement; dialogue opens up a wonderful opportunity to commit ourselves to a shared ministry. Engagement is far more important than agreement. The Social Principles can bring us together, even as opinions diverge.

How we teach is as important as what we teach; likewise, how we learn it is as important as what we learn. Our teaching and learning styles are influenced by our personalities. Use this opportunity to tailor learning and teaching to your own style and setting. Both you and the participants bring a wealth of lived experience, learned knowledge, and Christ-centered curiosity to your reading of the Social Principles.

Your goal, then, is to create a community of engaged learners. Support your participants as they speak from their hearts so that you can challenge their beliefs without shattering their value systems. Ask them to speak from personal life experience. Guide the group in knowing when it is inappropriate to overshadow another person's experience and when it is important to stand with those whose voices may not be in the room. Encourage people to use "I statements" (such as "I think," "I feel," or "I believe") rather than "you statements," which can foster assumptions and hurt feelings. When you emphasize dialogue and relationship over being "right," everyone's experience will be more rich and life-giving.

This guide is designed to walk your group through the Social Principles in six sessions. Each session should take about fifty minutes but can easily be condensed or expanded to fit the time allowed. The best way to prepare for this study is to familiarize yourself with this most recent edition of the Social Principles. If you are teaching a one-session overview, we recommend following the outline for the first session but using *Biblical Foundations* and *Dialogue* material from all six sessions, breaking into smaller groups as necessary.

SESSION OUTLINE

Creating Community (5 minutes)

The issues raised in the Social Principles can be controversial, and conversation has the potential to become contentious. As such, gathering the group and emphasizing the formation of a learning community is essential. In your first session, you will establish ground rules for conversation, which you will review in subsequent sessions. You may also use this time for introductions, review, and housekeeping reminders.

Biblical Foundations Exercises (10 minutes)

These exercises introduce group members to each section of the Social Principles and help them consider the way Scripture, as our primary source of theological reflection, has informed the construction of these social principles. Primarily discussion-based, this section can be done as a whole group or, if you have a large group, in groups of three or four.

Application (10 minutes)

Here you will work with a single social principle or a set of social principles to explore how they operate in our world and society. These activities engage various learning styles to deepen theological reflection and integration.

Dialogue (20 minutes)

A primary goal of the study of the Social Principles is to foster informed and respectful dialogue among people who may disagree (sometimes vehemently). We will use one of three communication exercises each week, as explained below. When instructed to read a statement from the Social Principles, read from the section you are discussing or a section from previous weeks. Take care in selecting statements; keep tabs on the group's dynamics: challenge when possible and lean back when the group needs a break.

Covenant (5 minutes)

We are a covenant community, dependent on God and on each other. Reserve a few minutes at the end of the session to affirm your commitment to this covenant and to your learning community. Reflect in silence. Ask each person to think of one main point that they will take away from the session. If time allows, have a few people share their take away. Some participants may want to share a commitment they have made in the session. Close with prayer.

Dialogue Exercise 1: Agree/Disagree

Ask participants to gather in the center of the room.

Say: *I will read a brief statement from the Social Principles. If you strongly agree with the statement, move to this side of the room.* (Indicate side.) *If you strongly disagree with the statement, move to this side of the room.* (Indicate opposite side.) *If you somewhat agree, somewhat disagree, or aren't sure (or don't want to say), pick a spot somewhere in the middle that best represents your thinking.*

Invite two or three people at various points on the spectrum to explain why they agree or disagree with the passage. Occasionally, when a sentence has a wide distribution of opinions, permit opportunities for representatives who agree and disagree to attempt to persuade the others of the wisdom of their position. Ask participants to listen carefully to the discussion. Invite them to empathize with a perspective that may not be their own. They should feel free to move within the room if their opinions change in the midst of the discussion. As you progress through the Social Principles, try to involve as many participants as possible in sharing their positions.

When meeting with adult groups, consider focusing first on five hot-button issues: immigration, capital punishment, abortion, human sexuality, and climate justice. With younger groups, you might target capital punishment, racial justice, prayer in schools, and the rights of children and youth.

During the discussion, you may ask follow-up questions. Examples include:

- *"If you were a delegate to General Conference and were faced with making a decision on the denomination's stance on _____, would you make your choice based on your personal opinion or the Church's current stance on the issue?"*
- *"What values, which interests, and whose needs do you think are reflected in our position on _____?"*
- *"According to the Social Principles, how should we respond to _____?"*
- *"How does _____ affect you and those closest to you?"*
- *"What can you and our congregation do to respond to the Social Principles on _____?"*
- *"Does this social principle have public policy implications? Which of these policy efforts do you support? Why?"*
- *"How will this exercise change your behavior and your commitments?"*

Encourage participants to articulate a biblical and theological basis for their beliefs and remind them that Wesleyan ethics rely on Scripture, reason, tradition, and experience as sources. The goal of the exercise is not debate but dialogue.

DIALOGUE EXERCISE 2: CONCENTRIC CIRCLES

This communication exercise works well with groups of eight or more and is easily adapted to fit the time you have available. Make sure that you allow enough time to state and respond to questions about the official positions of The United Methodist Church on these issues as addressed in the Social Principles. Suggested statements for use in this exercise begin on page 80.

Form a circle around the room. Have each alternate person step in to form a circle inside the bigger circle. The inner circle should face out so that everyone is looking at a partner in the opposite circle.

Say: *This exercise is based on the call in the preface to the Social Principles for "all members of The United Methodist Church" to engage in "prayerful, studied dialogue of faith and practice." Dialogue means there is room among United Methodists for honest, respectful differences of opinion. Everyone will not agree on each statement, and this is okay. We are trying to engage difficult issues but do so prayerfully, considering how we believe we should respond as people of faith. Try to suspend your judgment of what others share and to see the world through the eyes of the person to whom you are listening.*

I will read a statement pertaining to the Social Principles. The first partner will have forty-five seconds to share his or her thoughts. The sec-

ond partner will concentrate on listening; no interruptions. I will keep time. Then, the second partner will share, and the first will listen; again, no interruptions. I will then read a statement that explains how the Social Principles address the issue. The outer circle will rotate to the right so that everyone gets a new partner, and we repeat the process.

After all the statements you wish to explore have been discussed, form a single large circle. Ask: "What was it like to listen without responding? Was it difficult?" "Were some questions difficult to talk about?" "What did you learn about your partners?" Have the participants join hands, look around the circle, and make eye contact with the people with whom they have shared.

Dialogue Exercise 3: Wesleyan Quadrilateral

Discuss the Social Principles in light of the Wesleyan quadrilateral. In the 2016 *Discipline* ¶ 105, "Our Theological Task," pages 82-88, we are challenged to use "Scripture, tradition, experience, and reason" as tools for theological discernment and decision making. Place two pieces of masking tape on the floor in the shape of a cross. Label the four quadrants with these four sources (or simply assign a source to each corner of the room). Then read a sentence from the Social Principles. Ask participants to consider their position on the issue and then to move toward the quadrant they believe most supports their point of view. Discuss the reasons people made their choices.

SESSION ONE: INTRODUCTION AND THE NATURAL WORLD (¶ 160)

Creating Community: Ground Rules

Some topics covered in the Social Principles can be difficult to talk about. To encourage open and authentic dialogue, establish some ground rules before you begin. Ask: *What practices do we need to abide by in order to create a supportive learning environment?* Important points to cover include:

- Speak with respect.
- Use statements that begin with "I" ("I think," "I feel," "I believe," and so on) rather than statements that begin with "you."
- Share in a way that encourages dialogue and relationship.

- Be brief and to the point.
- Listen to understand one another's perspective.
- Recognize that people change their opinions based on life experience.
- Be open to being transformed by someone else's perspective.
- Try to stick with the conversation when it gets tough.
- Watch out for each other and take care of yourself.
- Trust that God is present in every relationship.

Introduction to the Social Principles

For many groups, participants will need a brief United Methodist polity lesson to understand how the Social Principles are adopted every four years. Read the description below or communicate the points in your own words.

The United Methodist Church is a global church: there are 12.8 million United Methodists worldwide. General Conference is the denomination's highest policy-making organization. It is a legislative body that meets every four years and is the only entity that can speak officially for The United Methodist Church. An equal number of clergy and lay delegates to General Conference are elected by each annual (or other regional) conference, relative to the number of United Methodists in their area. In 2016, 58% of General Conference delegates were from the U.S., 30% from Africa, 4.6% from Europe, and 5.5% from the Philippines. Annual conference delegates are chosen by each church. Bishops preside at General Conference but cannot vote.

General Conference considers petitions proposed by United Methodist individuals, groups, or agencies. Petitions are submitted in advance of General Conference. If supported, a petition amends the language of the *Book of Discipline*, the denomination's book of law. Though they are not church law, the Social Principles are included in the *Book of Discipline* and are amended in the same way as other portions of the *Discipline*. The Social Principles "are a prayerful and thoughtful effort on the part of the General Conference to speak to the human issues in the contemporary world from a sound biblical and theological foundation" (see preface).

Exploring the Social Principles

Cross the Line/Raise Your Card Exercise: This exercise will get participants thinking about issues raised in the Social Principles and help them begin to share about themselves. To begin, either have everyone form a straight line across the room, shoulder-to-shoulder or give everyone an index card. Read a statement from the list below. Participants are to respond if the statement is true and/or they agree with it by stepping forward or raising their index card. Encourage participants to listen silently, paying attention to how others respond to the statements. Choose ten to fifteen statements from the list below, remembering that you are trying to build trust and slowly challenge the group.

Say: *Please raise your card/step across the line silently if:*

1. You are the oldest [middle/youngest/only] child in your family.
2. You were raised in a farming or rural community.
3. Your first language was a language other than English.
4. You worked to pay for some or all of your education.
5. Your parents (or the people who raised you) were working class, did manual labor, or performed unskilled service work to make a living.
6. You have ever served in the military.
7. You have visited a mosque, synagogue, or house of worship other than a church.
8. You know someone who abuses or has abused alcohol or other drugs.
9. You know anyone who has died of a tobacco-related disease.
10. You know or have known someone living with HIV/AIDS.
11. You know or have known someone who has received an organ transplant.
12. You know someone who has had an abortion.
13. You know someone who self-identifies as gay, lesbian, bisexual, or transgender.
14. You have ever been bullied or have ever bullied someone else.
15. You have known someone who has survived domestic or gender violence.
16. You have experienced some form of racial injustice.
17. You know someone who has contemplated or completed suicide.
18. You have ever received preferential treatment because of your race.
19. You know anyone who has been incarcerated.
20. You have ever been part of a picket line or protest demonstration.

Reflection: Debrief the exercise in small groups or as a whole. Invite the group to listen carefully in order to deeply understand one another's perspectives.

1. What surprised you about your own or others' responses?
2. Were you ever the only one who raised your card or who crossed the line? How did that feel?
3. What was it like to notice others whose response was similar to your own?
4. Did you learn something new about someone in the exercise? Did you learn something new about yourself?
5. How might this exercise change your behavior in church and society?

The Natural World: Biblical Foundations

Read Genesis 1:26-30, followed by the opening paragraph of The Natural Word (¶ 160). Discuss the following questions as a group or in small groups of three or four.

1. Name the eight Social Principles listed in The Natural World.
2. What two major beliefs about God are stated in the introduction to this section?
3. What beliefs do you hold about God, the church, your community, and the planet that might help you decide what you, as a Christian, should do in response to these topics?
4. List the issues that the church says we stand for and support and those issues we stand against and want to change in The Natural World. Do you agree or disagree with the Social Principles? What would persuade you to change your mind or your behavior?
5. How can you advocate in church and society in favor of these Social Principles?

Dialogue

(Note: The Application activity is omitted from and the Dialogue time reduced in this session to allow time for group formation and introduction of the Social Principles.)

Lead the group through the Concentric Circles exercise outlined on page 64 using the statements pertinent to The Natural World (¶ 160). Concentric Circles statements begin on page 80.

Covenant

Reflect in silence. Ask each person to think of one main point she or he will take away from the session. If time allows, have a few people share their take away. Some participants may want to share a commitment they have made in the session. Close with prayer.

SESSION TWO: THE NURTURING COMMUNITY (¶ 161)

Creating Community

Review the ground rules your group set in the opening session. How did you do keeping to these agreements? Are there adjustments that need to be made to further encourage trust and authenticity?

Biblical Foundations

1. Read the introductory paragraph and review the eighteen Social Principles listed in The Nurturing Community.
2. Divide into three groups. Assign each group a Scripture: Romans 5:18–6:4; Luke 6:39-42; or Acts 2:43-47; 11:1-18. How does the Scripture relate to The Nurturing Community?
3. Read the statements in The Nurturing Community and discuss which ones you agree or disagree with and why.
4. Rewrite or revise a few of the Social Principles under The Nurturing Community from the perspective of someone who identifies as a youth, a person living in another country, or a person from another religious tradition.
5. Report back to the larger group what the experience of reading, discussing, and writing was like.

Application

Begin by looking at a mercy ministry in your church. Your church may collect and distribute food or clothes for a community pantry, provide meals to the unhoused, or participate in mission trips. These acts of face-to-face compassion are important, but it is essential to know the names of the people who are served by acts of mercy, to hear their stories, to learn about their communities, and to accompany them to advocate for sustainable solutions that address the cause of their immediate needs. This means we engage in acts of justice. The Social Principles point to acts of justice and direct us toward solutions that alleviate the source of people's suffering. As a group, brainstorm how you might expand this particular mercy ministry into a justice ministry as well. If there is momentum behind an idea, ask for a volunteer to talk with the pastor or missions chair about its potential.

Dialogue

Lead the group through the Wesleyan Quadrilateral exercise outlined on page 65 using statements from The Nurturing Community (¶ 161). Include statements from The Natural World as time allows.

Covenant

Reflect in silence. Ask each person to think of one main point she or he will take away from the session. If time allows, have a few people share their take away. Some participants may want to share a commitment they have made in the session. Close by praying in small groups for people directly impacted by a social principle in The Nurturing Community: survivors of bullying, depression, sexual assault; those who have experienced an unwelcome pregnancy and/or abortion; adoptive families; divorced families; and others.

SESSION THREE: THE SOCIAL COMMUNITY (¶ 162)

Creating Community

Review the ground rules your group set in the opening session. How did you do keeping to these agreements? Are there adjustments that need to be made to further encourage trust and authenticity?

Biblical Foundations

1. Read the introductory paragraph and several social principles in The Social Community. Note the four recurrent themes raised in this section: privileges, rights, human dignity, and responsibility.
2. Read Matthew 11:2-6 and Isaiah 40:1-11. Invite participants to write their immediate thoughts and feelings as they hear these Scriptures in the context of The Social Community section.
3. Share and highlight current news stories; if possible bring in visual images that convey recent headlines. Ask the

group to jot down instances of this section's social principles reflected in the news.

4. Ask the group:
   - "How do we secure vulnerable people's rights and dignity?"
   - "How do we use our privilege and responsibility to affirm that all persons are equally valuable in the sight of God?"
   - "What are the obstacles to achieving dignity and human rights for all?"
   - "What is the church doing to affirm each person's privileges, responsibilities, rights and dignity?"
5. Invite the group to pair off and choose one or two social principles from this section to commit to pursuing. Ask the pairs to check in weekly about how they are doing in engaging the selected social principle.

Application

Consider how an issue might affect your own child or a child you know well. We tend to be undisturbed when certain apparent injustices occur within society at large; however, we also tend to become protective in pursuit of greater rights on behalf of the children we know and love. For example, when considering "Rights of Women" in ¶ 162F, you might consider which of the rights mentioned in the Social Principles you want to see secured for your own daughter, granddaughter, or daughter of a close friend. Individually, write a letter or note to a child in your life, talking about your hopes for her or his rights and freedoms. Share in your small group (if you are comfortable doing so).

Dialogue

Lead the group through the Agree/Disagree exercise outlined on page 63 using statements from The Social Community (¶ 162). Include statements from The Natural World and The Nurturing Community as time allows.

Covenant

Reflect in silence. Ask each person to think of one main point she or he will take away from the session. If time allows, have a few people share their take away. Some participants may want to share a commitment they have made in the session. Close with prayer.

SESSION FOUR: THE ECONOMIC COMMUNITY (¶ 163)

Creating Community

Review the ground rules your group set in the opening session. How did you do keeping to these agreements? Are there adjustments that need to be made to further encourage trust and authenticity?

Biblical Foundations

1. Read the introductory paragraph and review the twelve Social Principles listed in The Economic Community section.
2. Divide into two groups. Have one group read Deuteronomy 10:17-18, 16:18-22; the other, Amos 8:4-8. Discuss each Scripture passage in light of The Economic Community section of the Social Principles.
3. Ask: "If you took the Social Principles with utmost seriousness, what changes, if any, would you need to make in your personal economic life?" "If we took the Social Principles found in The Economic Community seriously as a church, town, and nation, what changes would we need to make in our economic life together?" Brainstorm responses to these questions and the cost and benefits to making the suggested changes. Ask:
   - "Who would this impact?" "How would it impact them?"
   - "What incentives do we have as people, the church, and members of society to make those changes?"
   - "Which business and economic institutions can we partner with or challenge so that economic justice will flourish?"
4. Take an inventory of your local church or neighborhood to determine which of the Social Principles are most relevant and where you can make begin to create change.

Application

Reverse a reading. Assign portions of The Economic Community to individuals or small groups. Tell them to write a position that is the opposite of the one we find in the Social Principles. For example, in Section IV under "Gambling," it states, "As an act of faith and concern, Christians should abstain from gambling and should strive to minister to those victimized by the practice." A reverse reading might be, "As an act of lack of trust and uncaring, persons should gamble every chance they get, and should turn their backs on anyone gullible enough to lose their shirts and their grocery money." Discuss what life would be like if we were to live in opposition to the Social Principles.

Dialogue

Lead the group through the Wesleyan Quadrilateral exercise outlined on page 65 using the statements pertinent to The Economic Community (¶ 163). Include statements from The Social Community, The Nurturing Community, and The Natural World as time allows.

Covenant

Reflect in silence. Ask each person to think of one main point she or he will take away from the session. If time allows, have a few people share their take away. Some participants may want to share a commitment they have made in the session. Close with prayer.

SESSION FIVE: THE POLITICAL COMMUNITY (¶ 164)

Creating Community

Review the ground rules your group set in the opening session. How did you do keeping to these agreements? Are there adjustments that need to be made to further encourage trust and authenticity?

Biblical Foundations

1. Read Luke 4:16-19 and 1 Peter 2:17. Read the headings of the nine social principles in The Political Community section. Consider the vital functions of government for ordering a society.
2. Assign each participant (or small group, if applicable) one heading to read and summarize for the full group. After everyone has shared, ask:

- Did any principles surprise you? If so, was it in a positive or negative way? Why?
- How do you see these principles connecting with the life of our church and our community?
- Which principle seems the most controversial for the church today?

3. Discuss the meaning and practice of "Political Responsibility" (¶ 164B).

4. Discuss how The Political Community relates to The Natural World, The Nurturing Community, The Social Community, The Economic Community, and The World Community.

   Ask: If a community doesn't have political rights, how might they go about promoting social principles from the other areas?

5. Explain that some Christians believe that faith and politics do not go together. If this is the case, we may need to redefine both politics and faith. Ask:

   - "What is your first thought when you hear the term *politics* or *political*?"
   - "What is the role of Christians in impacting political change in favor of marginalized, oppressed, neglected and vulnerable peoples and communities?"
   - "How can United Methodists contribute to meaningful and respectful political discourse in nations and regions that are divided by political allegiances?"
   - "What gifts from Scripture and our tradition can guide us toward more fruitful discourse?"
   - "What rights do the Social Principles say we have that must be secured by governments?"

Application

Where do human rights come from? From a Christian perspective, we affirm that we are made in the Creator's image, so our best faith actions are reflections of God's activity in the world. By virtue of the dignity that comes with being born in the image of the Creator, we have inherent human rights. We have expanded our understanding of these rights over the years, but they continue to be rooted in our identity as bearers of the image of God.

Draw a simple stick figure and show it to the group. Ask: *"What rights can we associate with what we see in our own bodies? Are certain parts of our bodies indicative of particular human rights?"* Answers may include:

- Brain – A right to freedom of thought and conscience, a right to cultural expression, and a right to dissent.
- Mouth – A right to freedom of expression and speech.
- Nose and lungs – A right to a clean and sustainable environment.
- Heart – A right to love the person we love, a right to religious affiliation.
- Arms – A right to work and leisure, a right to collectively organize for workers' rights.
- Stomach – A right to quality food and water.
- Legs – A right to movement, to association, and to migration.
- Skin (ethnicity/racial identity) – A right not to be discriminated against, a right to ethnicity and racial identity, including indigenous identity.
- Entire body – A right not to enslaved, a right not to be socially harassed, a right not to be tortured, and a right to health care.

Ask: *"If we draw the body of an older adult, what additional social principles would be affirmed?"* (The rights to sufficient income; nondiscriminatory employment, educational, and service opportunities; access to medical care, and housing.)

Say: *"If we draw the body of a child, then we would include these particular rights: a right to shelter, clothing, and protection from economic, physical, emotional, and sexual exploitation and abuse. What rights are granted to adults but not to children?"* (The right to work, marry, vote, and own property.)

Ask: *"What happens when rights are denied? How can the church advocate for the rights in the public square?"*

Dialogue

Lead the group through the Concentric Circles exercise outlined on page 64 using the statements pertinent to The Political Community (¶ 164). Include statements related to previous sections of the Social Principles as time allows. Concentric Circles statements begin on page 80.

Covenant

Reflect in silence. Ask each person to think of one main point she or he will take away from the session. If time allows, have a few people share their take away. Some participants may want to share a commitment they have made in the session. Close with prayer.

SESSION SIX: THE WORLD COMMUNITY (¶ 165)

Creating Community

Review the ground rules your group set in the opening session. How did you do keeping to these agreements? Are there adjustments that need to be made to further encourage trust and authenticity?

Biblical Foundations

1. Read and compare Lamentations 3:23-33; Acts 17:26; and 1 Peter 2:9.
2. Invite the group to look at these three Scriptures in light of the four World Community social principles.
3. Ask:
   - "What examples can you think of in which international and multilateral cooperation by governments or by nongovernmental groups have made a definite advance in improving the world community?"
   - "In what ways has The United Methodist Church helped initiate sustainable expressions of reconciliation, conflict transformation, and peace-building across cultures and nations?"
   - "What values and needs do these social principles promote and respond to?"

Application

Invite participants to learn more about the United Nations' Sustainable Development Goals (SDGs) and how they align with the goals stated in The World Community. (Information on the SDGs is available at www.un.org.)

Say: *In 2015, members of the United Nations adopted a set of goals to end poverty, to protect the planet, and to ensure prosperity for all. The new "Sustainable Development Goals" (SDGs) have specific targets to be achieved over the next fifteen years, which include:*
   - Ending extreme poverty
   - Creating affordable and clean energy and a sustainable climate

- Eliminating hunger around the world
- Creating decent work and economic growth
- Promoting good health and well-being
- Engaging in industry, innovation, and infrastructure
- Caring for life on land and underwater
- Ensuring quality education
- Reducing inequalities
- Promoting peace, justice, and strong institutions
- Advocating for gender equality, sustainable communities, clean water and sanitation
- Responsible consumption and production

In what ways do the United Methodist Social Principles mirror the SDGs? What does the church contribute to our understanding and application of the SDGs?

Dialogue

Lead the group through the Concentric Circles exercise outlined on page 64 using the statements pertinent to The World Community (¶ 165). Include statements related to previous sections of the Social Principles as time allows. Concentric Circles statements begin on page 80.

Covenant

Reflect in silence. Ask each person to think of one main point she or he will take away from the session. If time allows, have a few people share their take away. Some participants may want to share a commitment they have made in the session. Close with prayer for each of the regions where The United Methodist Church is engaging in ministry, advocacy, and mission.

ADDITIONAL ACTIVITIES

Most of the teaching suggestions offered here can work with any of the Social Principles. The key is to find several different approaches that work well with your group members and to mix the methods so that persons with different learning styles have a greater chance to learn and engage with the Social Principles.

A. Put a section under a "microscope." Ask your group members to work through one section sentence by sentence. Write down the topic of the sentence. Determine what the section is in favor of and what it is against. See if you can find a statement supporting a particular position. Does the social principle give an explicit reason for its conclusion? Does that reason appeal to particular United Methodist beliefs or practices? If so, what are they?

B. Hear some living history. Older adults are rich resources for understanding changes that have taken place over decades. If several generations of adults are represented in your class, provide time for the older members to share about changes that have taken place within their lifetimes with regard to a social justice issue. For example, if one of your older members is a lifelong union member, he or she likely will be able to talk about changes in labor-management relations, collective bargaining, and the standard of living for workers. If your group members are mostly under fifty years old, recruit a panel of older adults to share their memories about some social issues. One possibility is to invite guests of different racial, ethnic, or religious backgrounds but of the same generation to talk about changes in civil and human rights.

C. Write a petition to the 2020 General Conference. If most or all of the members of your class would like to see a portion of the Social Principles changed, help them research how to prepare a petition to send to General Conference. Encourage them to submit their petition. At the next General Conference, your participants can track their petitions through your conference's delegates. If not everyone agrees on changing a single social principle, encourage the group to form petition interest groups. In so doing, participants will have to research a specific social issue thoroughly enough to be able to take an informed position on it, learn the process to submit a petition to General Conference, and take a firm stand on an issue, backing it up with action, all of which is excellent advocacy training.

D. Read current newspapers and social media posts. Bring a week's worth of news stories, both local and global. Ask group members to gather news from a variety of sources and to compare how they each tell the same story. How does the author or publication's social location affect their retelling of the story? How should this shape our consumption of information?

E. Audit your local church. Assign portions of the Social Principles to individuals or small groups to investigate how seriously your church takes this principle. For example, do you strive to "support a more ecologically equitable and sustainable world leading to a higher quality of life for all of God's creation" and still use foam cups or coffee that is not fair trade during coffee time (¶ 160)? Can a church be said to take seriously the section on tobacco and permit persons to smoke inside its building? How do we live faithfully in the tension between theory and practice? If group members can suggest specific policy changes, encourage them to present their ideas to the church council, the board of trustees, or the appropriate decision-making body.

F.   Bring an issue into your own backyard. An issue becomes more urgent when it affects the people near and dear to us. When we can put a face, story, and name to an issue, the social principle becomes a matter of utmost importance. Assign individual social principles to groups of two to four persons. Ask them to localize the issue spoken about in their section. For example, under the section on "Water, Air, Soil, Minerals, Plants" in The Natural World, participants might know of a toxic waste facility planned for their neighborhood or region. Encourage them to find out more about the issue. How do the Social Principles shed light on that particular toxic waste facility?

G.   Explore an unfamiliar topic. Some social justice issues might be new or seem irrelevant to members of your group. For example, an urban congregation may not readily identify with the section on "Rural Life," and many of us may not know much about genetic technology or fair trade products. Assign such topics to group members to research and report to the group the following week. Go in-depth: invite guest presenters; take a field trip; immerse yourself in another cultural context.

H.   Give your group a chance to teach and mentor others. One of the most effective ways to understand a topic is to prepare to teach it to someone else. Have your group teach (or prepare lessons for someone else to teach) the Social Principles to another group, such as such as a class of youth, the church trustees, or the missions committee. Remind your group members that they need to tailor their teaching to the needs of the learners.

I.   Educate, advocate, and organize. Focus on a social principle the group is passionate about. Research the social principle and advocate for it through letter writing campaigns, e-mails, phone calls, and face-to-face visits with your local, state, and national legislators. Network with other local churches, your conference Board of Church and Society, and like-minded community members to stand up for justice and peace.

Suggested Statements for Concentric Circle Dialogue

1.   Climate change is a myth. The planet was around long before us, and we have a responsibility to make a profit by any means necessary. The more natural resources we use, the better. Besides, how else do you expect nations to develop if they don't power their industry through coal and oil?
     Social Principles: "We therefore support efforts of all governments to require mandatory reductions in greenhouse gas emissions and call on individuals, congregations, businesses, industries, and communities to reduce their emissions" (¶ 160D).

2.   It is perfectly reasonable to believe that both the biblical account of creation and the theory of evolution are legitimate explanations of how the world came to be what it is today.
     Social Principles: "We preclude science from making authoritative claims about theological issues and theology from making authoritative claims about scientific issues. We find that science's descriptions of cosmological, geological, and biological evolution are not in conflict with theology" (¶ 160F).

3.   It has been said that nobody is an island, and no one is really complete until they find a life partner and friend.
     Social Principles: "We affirm the integrity of single persons, and we reject all social practices that discriminate or social attitudes that are prejudicial against persons because they are single" (¶ 161E).
     Social Principles: "We especially reject the idea that God made individuals as incomplete fragments, made whole only in union with another" (¶ 161F).

4.   Women do well in pastoral ministry and leadership at all levels of the church and society if given a fair chance. Many people just won't give them a chance.

Social Principles: "We affirm with Scripture the common humanity of male and female, both having equal worth in the eyes of God" (¶ 161F).

5. Sexual abuse is real, and it's wrong. But we just shouldn't keep taking about it. If we stop bringing the problem up, it will go away.

   Social Principles: "Violent, disrespectful, or abusive sexual expressions do not confirm sexuality as God's good gift. We reject all sexual expressions that damage the humanity God has given us as birthright, and we affirm only that sexual expression that enhances that same humanity" (¶ 161I).

6. Hazing and bullying is part of life. Let people work it out between themselves. The church cannot do much to stop it, so we should not even try.

   Social Principles: "Bullying is a growing problem in parts of the connection. It is a contributing factor in suicide and in the violence we see in some cultures today. We affirm the right of all people, regardless of gender, socioeconomic status, race, religion, disability, age, physical appearance, sexual orientation and gender identity, to be free of unwanted aggressive behavior and harmful control tactics" (¶ 161R).

7. Racism, like sexism, is just something we need to accept. It's human nature. Learn to live with it and move on.

   Social Principles: "Racism is the combination of the power to dominate by one race over other races and a value system that assumes that the dominant race is innately superior to the others. Racism includes both personal and institutional racism. Personal racism is manifested through the individual expressions, attitudes, and/or behaviors that accept the assumptions of a racist value system and that maintain the benefits of this system. Institutional racism is the established social pattern that supports implicitly or explicitly the racist value system. Racism, manifested as sin, plagues and hinders our relationship with Christ, inasmuch as it is antithetical to the gospel itself" (¶ 162A).

8. Religious differences can bring us closer together or they can pull us apart. We need to respect our religious differences and work together to lift each other up, not pull each other down.

   Social Principles: "We condemn all overt and covert forms of religious intolerance, being especially sensitive to their expression in media stereotyping. We assert the right of all religions and their adherents to freedom from legal, economic, and social discrimination" (¶ 162B).

9. Young people often make horrible decisions. It's safer, wiser, and easier if responsible, caring adults just make all decisions for them.
Social Principles: "Our society is characterized by a large population of young people who frequently find full participation in society difficult. Therefore, we urge development of policies that encourage inclusion of young people in decision-making processes and that eliminate discrimination and exploitation" (¶ 162D).

10. A little tobacco smoke never hurt anybody. Smoking a pipe or cigar is certainly not as bad as smoking cigarettes. It's my choice.
Social Principles: "In light of the overwhelming evidence that tobacco smoking and the use of smokeless tobacco are hazardous to the health of persons of all ages, we recommend total abstinence from the use of tobacco" (¶ 162M).

11. I know that some poor people don't have health insurance, but they have clinics they can go to. We simply cannot afford for everyone to have access to health care when they need it.
Social Principles: "Health care is a basic human right. . . . It is unjust to construct or perpetuate barriers to physical or mental wholeness or full participation in community" (¶ 162V).

12. Mental illness is a reality. We are just too uncomfortable to bring it up in church. People are ashamed of being stigmatized and labeled.
Social Principles: "Persons with mental illness and their families have a right to be treated with respect on the basis of common humanity and accurate information. They also have a right and responsibility to obtain care appropriate to their condition. The United Methodist Church pledges to foster policies that promote compassion, advocate for access to care, and eradicate stigma within the Church and in communities" (¶ 162X).

13. It's God's will that some countries should have more than other countries and that strong countries have a right to use the natural resources of poor countries to get wealthier. Try-

ing to redistribute wealth undermines the will of God; some of us are meant to get rich while others are meant to stay poor.

Social Principles: "As a church, we are called to support the poor and challenge the rich." Also, "In order to provide basic needs such as food, clothing, shelter, education, health care, and other necessities, ways must be found to share more equitably the resources of the world" (¶ 163E).

14. Migrant workers are not treated with dignity and are denied their human rights. The deck is stacked against their having a fair shake because everyone knows they can't go running to the police or the government if they aren't treated fairly.

    Social Principles: "We call upon governments and all employers to ensure for foreign workers the same economic, educational, and social benefits enjoyed by other citizens" (¶ 163F).

15. A little gambling for small amounts of money is fun and should be allowed in our churches and fellowship halls, like bingo night.

    Social Principles: "Gambling is a menace to society, deadly to the best interests of moral, social, economic, and spiritual life, destructive of good government and good stewardship" (¶ 163G).

16. Corporations have one responsibility: to make a profit any way they can for their shareholders.

    Social Principles: "Corporations are responsible not only to their stockholders, but also to other stakeholders: their workers, suppliers, vendors, customers, the communities in which they do business, and for the earth, which supports them" (¶ 163I).

17. The problem with capital punishment is that it doesn't cover enough crimes; people would think twice about breaking the law if they knew the consequence.

    Social Principles: "We oppose the death penalty (capital punishment) and urge its elimination from all criminal codes" (¶ 164G).

18. The only fair way to get people to serve in the military is to bring back the draft. Unless we do that, we're not going to have enough people to serve.

    Social Principles: "We reject national policies of enforced military service as incompatible with the gospel" (¶ 164I).

19. The church has been an outspoken critic of violence in all its forms. That must include war. There has to be a better way of solving problems in the twenty-first century than relying on violent conflict to bring about peace.

    Social Principles: "We believe war is incompatible with the teachings and example of Christ" (¶ 165C).

20. One way to prevent new wars and to promote better lives for people around the world is to establish basic laws that apply to all nations and then to figure out a way to enforce them, no exceptions.

    Our Social Creed: "We dedicate ourselves to peace throughout the world, to the rule of justice and law among nations, and to individual freedom for all people of the world" (¶ 166).

RESOURCES

Unless otherwise noted, all resources are available at www.cokesbury.com.

The Book of Discipline of The United Methodist Church. Updated and published by The United Methodist Publishing House following each General Conference. Pay particular attention to the sections on local church ministry and General Board of Church and Society. The Social Principles are Part V, ¶¶ 160–166.

The Book of Resolutions of The United Methodist Church. Updated and published by The United Methodist Publishing House after each General Conference. Includes social-concerns statements for consideration and action by all United Methodists.

Faith and Facts Cards. Four-color, worship-bulletin-size cards that address a variety of subjects. Topics include health care, domestic violence, criminal justice reform, HIV/AIDS, human trafficking, death penalty, climate justice, living wage, alcohol and other drugs, gambling, hunger and poverty, and U.S. immigration. Available at www.umcjustice.org.

Guidelines Church & Society: Advocate and Witness for Peace and Justice. A 30-page booklet that provides a practical biblical and theological basis for social justice ministry. Covers the role of boards of church and society in local churches and conferences; cultivating the spiritual disciplines of social justice action, reflection, and leadership development through relationships of advocacy and organizing.

Living Our Principles. A six-episode DVD film series that illustrates how United Methodists put into practice the Social Principles. Each episode focuses on a different section of the Social Principles and the people who live them out through education, advocacy, and organizing. Available at www.umcjustice.org.

United Methodist Communications website (umcom.org). Download-able media and print resources to support United Method-ist Special Sundays that pertain to the Social Principles: Hu-man Relations Day and Peace with Justice Sunday.

United Methodist Seminars on National and International Affairs

These seminars are educational, interactive, faith-forming, thought-provoking, and fun. Seminars are tailor-made for each group, which selects the topic. The design team at the General Board of Church and Society creates a seminar to answer questions, challenge assumptions, and open the group to reflection on the chosen issues. United Method-ist Seminars take place at the United Methodist Building on Capitol Hill adjacent to the Supreme Court and the U.S. Capitol. In addition, United Methodist Women organizes U.N. seminars that take place at the Church Center for the United Nations across the street from the U.N. headquar-ters. For Washington, D.C. seminars, sponsored by General Board of Church and Society, call (202) 488-5609. For United Nations seminars, sponsored by United Methodist Women, call (212) 682-3633.

INDEX